About the Author

Rodney Ellis's working career was spent entirely in computing, including time both as a software engineer, and a university lecturer. Throughout this, he developed an increasing interest in history; eventually, after retirement, this was reinforced by first and second degrees in classics awarded by the Open University. His specific interest is classical Athens, with particular emphasis on the Athenian navy and its significance to the classical period.

How the Trireme Brought Democracy to Athens

Rodney Ellis

How the Trireme Brought Democracy to Athens

Vanguard Press

VANGUARD PAPERBACK

© Copyright 2024
Rodney Ellis

The right of Rodney Ellis to be identified as author of
this work has been asserted by him in accordance with the
Copyright, Designs and Patents Act 1988.

All Rights Reserved

No reproduction, copy or transmission of this publication
may be made without written permission.
No paragraph of this publication may be reproduced,
copied or transmitted save with the written permission of the publisher, or in
accordance with the provisions
of the Copyright Act 1956 (as amended).

Any person who commits any unauthorised act in relation to this publication
may be liable to criminal prosecution and civil claims for damages.

A CIP catalogue record for this title is available from the British Library.

ISBN 978-1-83794-238-1

The interpretation of the events described in this book is entirely the
responsibility of the author.

Vanguard Press is an imprint of
Pegasus Elliot Mackenzie Publishers Ltd.
www.pegasuspublishers.com

First Published in 2024

Vanguard Press
Sheraton House Castle Park
Cambridge England

Printed & Bound in Great Britain

Dedication

To my family

Introduction

The *Glory That Was Greece* has informed and inspired western culture from the Renaissance to the present day, perhaps most frequently symbolised by a view of the ruins of the Parthenon, still overpoweringly impressive in its commanding nobility. Although the phrase refers to the entire country, virtually everything encapsulated in it originated during a brief period – less than a century – in only one of the several hundred city-states that made up what we now know as Greece – a name bestowed by the Romans and unknown at the time of its greatness. The city in question was Athens, and the historical period was the later part of the fifth century BC. The culture of Athens during this period, often referred to as classical, provided a model which combined magnificent architecture and artistic achievements with a polity that is probably an inimitable paradigm for similarly inspired systems ever since. This book attempts to explain how this culture developed its final form and was maintained by a complex and, in some senses, paradoxical nexus of influences.

The most significant influence on classical culture was the political regime under which it flourished. This took the form of a democracy – the rule of the people – one moreover of a particularly pure, or extreme, nature. The development of this system occurred in stages over one and a half centuries and forms one of the major themes of this book. It is arguable that the duration of this extended process enabled the eventual establishment of democracy in a relatively peaceful manner. In this, Athens was unusual in that many Greek states installed democratic regimes, but by violent revolution, with the poor rising against the rich, invariably followed by equally violent counter-revolutions. There was never any popular uprising to enforce material equality by dispossessing the rich throughout the period of democratic rule that lasted towards the end of the third century BC, despite the very considerable material inequalities in Athenian society. The democracy, however, did provide equality in the form of both equality before the law for all citizens and equality of the right to be heard in the ekklesia, or assembly, where all male citizens who wished to attend voted on a wide variety of matters of state, from declarations of war to the prosecution of significant individuals such as military leaders. Female citizens could not attend the ekklesia. (It should be pointed out that the population of classical Athens was by no means comprised only of its citizens: there were many foreigners, many of whom were, of course, Greek, who were permitted to live in the state, known as Metics, and who had certain rights but not those of citizens. There were also many slaves who had no civic rights.) There is some evidence that for the great majority of the citizenship, particularly those of the lower classes, democracy was a unifying source of pride. The attitudes of the upper classes were more varied; many of the wealthy contributed willingly to the state; on the other hand, there was probably always a significant minority of oligarchs who were never reconciled to the democracy and on two occasions, this became sufficiently empowered to overthrow the democracy for brief periods. The mention of classes is perhaps surprising in the context of radical democracy, but one of the paradoxes of the culture was the existence of, nominally at least, a well-defined system of classes to one of which every citizen was defined as belonging, but which in practice had no effect on the equalities mentioned above.

The city-state of Athens extended over the province of Attica, which borders on the north coast of the Saronic Gulf at its eastern end and on the strait running northwest between the mainland and the island of Euboea. The Gulf runs from the Aegean Sea to the Isthmus of Corinth, the narrow strip of land that separates the Saronic from the Corinthian Gulf, thus preventing the Peloponnese, to the south, from being a true island. Athens' neighbouring states included, to the north west of Atttica, Boeotia and its historic city, Thebes. Adjoining Attica along the coast of the Gulf, going west, lay Eleusis, which had been incorporated into the Athenian state, then the small state of Megara, and then close to the southern end of the Isthmus, and near its west coast was situated Corinth. The island state of Aegina lay across the Saronic Gulf to the South West of Athens. Much of the land over which the province extended was mountainous and was generally not especially fertile, even though much of it was under cultivation, largely devoted to vines or olives. Significantly, those who lived in the country areas of

Attica and possessed the relevant qualifications of birth were Athenian citizens with the same rights as the city-dwellers. Athens' geographic situation was not insignificant to the trajectory of its cultural development, particularly its proximity to the sea – the city of Athens was located some five miles inland from its port, the Piraeus – giving it ready access to the Aegean and the Ionic coast, then described as Asia; now known as Asia Minor.

This accessibility to the Aegean and Asia was a contributory factor to a period of threatened and actual warfare involving Athens during the first part of the fifth century BC. There was nothing unusual in a Greek state being in a state of war, often with other Greek states. And as another paradox, the fifth century saw Athens in such a state continually up to 431 BC, apart from a brief lull in the four hundred and forties, and then continuously for most of the next twenty-seven years, in other words, for much of the classical era. The warfare of the first two decades, however, was unique in that it both established Athens as the saviour of Greece and also initiated a profound re-orientation of Athens towards becoming a *thalassocracy* – a maritime power – which also had a significant stimulus to the development of the democracy. The development of this thalassocracy forms another theme of this book.

The conflict in the first decades of the fifth century BC pitted Athens against two of the 'Great Kings' of Persia: Darius and his successor, Xerxes. Shortly after the turn of the century, the 'Ionian' Greek city-states located on or near the eastern coast of the Aegean revolted against

Persian rule. In this, they were supported by a number of mainland Greek states, of which the most important was Athens, which had cultural ties with many of them, some of whom had significant numbers of Athenian settlers. Athens frequently claimed to be an Ionian city, even though it was located on the mainland. The revolt was crushed by the Persians, and any Athenian presence was withdrawn; however, their support for the Ionians did not go unnoticed by Darius, the current Persian king, and he determined to mount a punitive expedition to exact revenge on the Greeks, particularly the Athenians. This took the form of a sea-borne force, which landed near Athens at Marathon. The Athenians had been forewarned of this attack and had assembled as large a force that they could muster, which was waiting when the Persians attempted to land. Their determined defence prevented the Persians from landing in good order, and the survivors were eventually pursued back to their ships, and the defeated force sailed back to Asia. This, of course, did nothing to assuage the hatred of Athens on the part of the Persian monarchy.

The fact that the assault had been an amphibious one and that the crushing of the Ionian revolt had also involved Persian naval forces was not lost on the Athenians, particularly one individual, Themistocles. He was a leading figure in Athenian political life and was thus in a position to influence strategic thought in the state, and he became convinced of the need for Athens, which currently possessed few warships, to equip herself with a powerful navy, initially for essentially defensive reasons. Although this view was by no means accepted unanimously, it eventually prevailed, and in the next decade, Athens built up a fleet of warships of a size comparable with established Greek naval powers such as Corinth and Corcyra. A significant stimulus to this activity was the threat of a new attack from Persia, where Darius' successor Xerxes had inherited his hatred of the Greeks, and the Athenians particularly, and had made no secret of the fact that he was building up a huge force, on both land and sea, to impose Persian rule over the Greek mainland, mirroring that over the Ionian Greek states, and with an initial objective of destroying Athens. When the Persian fleet was eventually confronted by a far smaller Greek fleet, which was comprised largely of Athenian ships, the result was victory for the Greeks. The effect on Xerxes, who witnessed the battle, was profound, and he returned to Persia with most of his huge land army, leaving behind a relatively smaller force that was finally defeated some months later.

Athens' leadership in the defeat of the Persian invasions led to her assuming a commanding role in a defensive alliance of Greek states, created to deter and indeed reverse the threat from Persia, which continued to smoulder for several more decades. The story of how this alliance developed and changed its nature, with large-scale effects on democracy and, indeed, classical culture, is, again, a major theme of this book. Suffice it to say that, as the century wore on, the Athenian state became ever more wealthy and powerful, to such an extent as to provoke both jealousy and fear in other large states. Foremost amongst these were the Spartans, who had long considered themselves, with some justification, the hegemon of Greece. They were certainly leaders of a loose alliance of Peloponnesian states, including some geographically close to Athens, including Corinth, Megara and Aegina. Despite having signed a peace treaty for thirty years with Athens in the mid four hundred and forties, the Spartans' antagonism grew steadily over the next decade until it became clear that only a dramatic diminution of Athens' power would satisfy them and that only warfare could achieve this. After a considerable period of claims and counter-claims about the peace treaty being broken, war was tacitly declared, for which Sparta's pretext was the claim that they were fighting to 'free the Greeks,' by implication accusing Athens of enslaving her allies. An accusation with which some of them would have concurred. This war, which began in four hundred and thirty-one BC, is known historically as the Peloponnesian War. It continued until four hundred and four BC, with a brief break in four hundred and twenty-two. In both phases of the war, the Athenians, although generally having the upper hand due to their naval superiority, experienced disasters that might have been expected to have forced them to sue for peace, but the democracy exhibited quite remarkable powers of resilience, until the final one which, tellingly, resulted in the loss of the greater part of the whole Athenian fleet and, in a short time, their capitulation.

Although the war was lost and the democracy overthrown, by yet a further demonstration of the resilience of the democratic spirit in Athens, the democracy was re-established, albeit as a shadow of its former self.

Chapter 1
The Roots of Athenian Democracy

The city-state, or *polis*, of Athens, consisted of an area of what is now known as Greece, forming the province of Attica, a region of generally poor quality farmland bounded by mountains, the Aegean Sea and the Saronic Gulf near the edge of which lay the city of Athens. As Greece emerged from the so-called dark age, roughly the tenth and ninth centuries BC, which followed the collapse of the Mycaean palace-based civilisation, Attica contained a number of small independent sovereignties, one of which, the most powerful, ruled the city of Athens from a commanding redoubt known as the Acropolis (the 'high city'). The Lords of the Acropolis conducted a policy of gradual subjugation of these sovereignties, eventually uniting the whole of Attica under what has been called a 'loose overlordship' of Athens. With the passage of time, the minor lordships under this arrangement, motivated by what seems to have been a growing sentiment for unification, abandoned their independence and became merged into a single community governed by the city of Athens. This merging was so complete that Athenian citizenship, with its associated political rights, was not restricted to the inhabitants of the city but applied to every inhabitant of Attica, even in relatively remote villages, provided they met the requirements of citizenship. The Athenian citizenry in this united community comprised three distinct classes: the *eupatridai* – the aristocrats, who were generally large land owners; the *georgoi* – the peasant farmers with small land holdings, and the *demiurgoi* – who engaged in trade or commerce and were typically city dwellers. Outside these classes, there were landless agricultural labourers, known as *hektemorai*, or 'sixth-parters,' who worked for a sixth part of what they produced, and the various artisans and assistants who were employed by the *demiurgoi*, and there were also foreigners permitted to live in Attica, who were known as *metics*. All these were free men, in the sense of not being slaves; however, they were not citizens and were not permitted to attend the citizen assembly, the *ekklesia*.

The government of the Athenian state up to and probably including the *Synoecism*, or unifying, of Attica was a monarchy, presumably absolute in its nature, but apparently, fairly soon after the Synoecism, it became modified by the introduction of non-royal posts: the *polemarch*, or military commander, and the *Archon* who was the chief magistrate. These posts were initially appointments for life made by the aristocracy and can be seen as a successful attempt to distribute power from the monarchy to that class, with the role of the king being reduced to a largely religious significance. As such, it existed well into the democracy of the fifth century, by which time it had become a position occupied by an elected candidate each year. This change from monarchy to what was effectively a republic was very early in comparison to similar changes in other Greek states, and its republican nature was strengthened in the eighth century BC by the restriction of the duration of the appointment of the archon from 'for life' to ten years, then subsequently in the seventh century to one year. At its inception, the post of Archon was chosen from the members of one pre-eminent family, the Medontids, but this also had changed by the time of the adoption of the annual election, for which any member of the *eupatridae* could be put forward. The archon ruled with the assistance of a council of elders, all of whom were aristocrats, which became known as the Council of the Areopagus, named after the hill on which it met, which was close to the Acropolis and also the Pnyx, which was another hill close by where the ekklesia met.

At the time of the synoecism, Athenian society was almost exclusively occupied with agriculture, and thus the class system, while fundamentally enshrining the distinction of the aristocracy, defined by their noble birth, from the rest, was essentially determined by land holding, with the aristocracy, as noted previously, being distinguished by their large estates, held by generations of powerful clans. The seventh and sixth centuries BC saw a slow but significant increase in trade between Athens and other Greek states, largely supported by sea traffic, for which Athens possessed the invaluable resource of the natural harbour of the Bay of Phaleron, only a few miles from the city. This produced a weakening in connection with agriculture in that some aristocrats, despite a general contempt for commerce, were attracted by the considerable wealth that successful trading could generate and so engaged in enterprises hitherto seen as the province of the *demiurgoi*. In consequence, as the result of the varying outcomes to which any speculative trading is prone, some became (more) wealthy, while others suffered losses so that the relationship between wealth and aristocracy and land holding became less fixed. This tendency was also amplified as some of the *demiurgoi* also became wealthy, to the extent of being able to purchase large estates, probably from aristocrats who had been unlucky or unwise in their commercial ventures. It then became clear that class distinctions based simply on birth and ancestral land holdings were no longer adequate; what was required was a straightforward indication of wealth, which had become the principal criterion for entry into the government of the state. Public office was an expensive pastime to which none but the wealthy could aspire. And so, a new set of classes based on wealth was adopted, which was still related to land holding but defined in terms of the wealth it produced, measured in amounts of agricultural produce. Thus, members of the highest class, the *pentakosiomedimnoi*, owned land capable of producing five hundred bushels of dry crops, probably grain or its equivalent in olive oil or wine. The second highest, the *hippeis,* and the third, the *zeugitai*, also had volumes of annual production set as their qualifying limits; however, the only evidence for these quantities is found in Aristotle, who was writing some two centuries after their promulgation, and recent convincing analysis has cast doubt on their veracity. For both the *hippeis* and the *zeugitai*, however, alternative property qualifications were established, which provided straightforward criteria for their characterisation.

The *hippeis*, or knights, as the term has been generally translated, were distinguished as owning one or more horses and maintaining them at a sufficient level, together with the necessary harness and weaponry to be able to fight as cavalrymen. The fighting capability was obviously age-dependent and also limited by the relatively small cavalry forces that the Athenians conventionally used, and the essential requirement associated with the class was that of supporting the not-inconsiderable financial burden of horse ownership.

The zeugitai, a term derived from the Greek for 'yoke,' were required to possess a pair of oxen, a qualification effectively defining them as farmers with sufficient land to necessitate ploughing – for which a yoked pair was typically required. The zeugitai have often been identified as the 'hoplite class' that is the main source of recruitment of the heavily armed soldiers, the hoplites, who formed the core of the military in most Greek states. While there is clear evidence to support the association of the zeugitai with hoplite service, it would be wrong to regard this association as exclusive, as there is also evidence of hoplite service undertaken by members of all three and later four classes.

The fourth class alluded to contained all those free men such as the hektemorai, farmers who failed to meet the requirements of the zeugitai and the many journeymen or workless in the city. These were lumped together, forming a fourth and lowest class known as the *thetes*: a perhaps brutally honest nomenclature borrowed from the general term for a hired labourer. The thetes did not possess any of the political rights of citizens and were not permitted to attend the ekklesia.

Greek city-states, foreshadowing those in more recent times such as in late medieval Italy, existed in a perpetual state of competition, usually warlike, with frequent raiding parties or more serious attempts at full-scale invasion. In consequence, the maintenance of an adequate defence capability was essential to the continuing independent existence of every city-state. It might be noted that Plato, in the fourth century BC and hardly an unreconstructed warmonger, insisted on the necessity of a defence force in the ideal state depicted in his *Laws*, despite the fact that its population was to be restricted to five thousand (male) citizens. Very soon after the emergence of the *polis,* the idea of citizenship, inculcating loyalty to a community rather than to a clan, appears to have developed, and with it, that of joint responsibility for defence rather than the reliance on a cast of aristocratic heroes familiar to the Greeks from the epics of Homer. This idea came to fruition in the 'hoplite revolution' where the citizens of city-states, particularly those who could afford the relatively costly 'panoply' consisting mainly of a shield and one or more spears, and possibly a helmet, formed themselves into well-disciplined lines, with overlapping shields. These *phalanxes* then constituted the defensive and offensive arms of their respective cities when their rivalries and quarrels reached the stage of armed conflict. The duration of these conflicts, which consisted of the two opposing phalanxes approaching each other and engaging, using a combination of shoving and spear thrusting, was generally short, as the first side to lose their formation and break would be unlikely to be able to reform in the face of the other, unbroken, force, and generally took to flight. What was significantly absent from phalanx warfare was the opportunity for displays of individual daring, for such would inevitably destroy the integrity and linearity of the 'wall of shields.' Thus the phalanx both relied on and symbolised the submerging of the individual in the communal effort of the defence or the projection of the power of the state. It is a fact of considerable significance that the undoubted courage that was required of the hoplite members of the phalanx became the exclusive model for military courage, even in the fifth century BC when phalanx warfare was comparatively rare. The seventh-century poet Tyrtaeus was celebrated, particularly by the Spartans, for his characterisation of courage in terms of the clash of the phalanxes:

'But getting in close where fighting is hand to hand, inflicting a wound

With his long spear or sword, taking the enemy's life,
With his foot planted alongside the foot and his shield pressed against the shield.'

Tyrtaeus' depiction calls into question some fairly recent accounts of phalanx warfare as a somewhat more lethal Rugby scrum.

As noted above, the phalanx depended upon the communal endeavour of its members for its success, with no distinction of rank or authority – equality, in other words – and this has become the basis for the suggestion that the 'hoplite revolution,' which grew out of the development of the polis, formed the basis of a tendency in the city-states *(poleis)* to recognise a degree of equality within the (male) citizen body, arising from their shared military experience – as a 'guild of warriors.'

Although aristocrats certainly took their place in the phalanx, probably distinguished by their ornate panoplies, as noted above, the great majority of the hoplites were zeugitai, who formed a large segment of the Athenian citizenry and who could afford the minimal necessary armament. It should be noted that this financial requirement was sufficient to exclude the thetes from the 'guild of warriors.' They were, however, able to contribute to military activities as *peltasts*, who undertook an auxiliary role on the side-lines of the phalanx confrontation, throwing a variety of missiles of a variety of types, including darts and stones, usually employing a hit-and-run tactic. As such, they were not regarded as exhibiting true military virtue.

Towards the end of the seventh century BC, despite the general recognition of the dependence of the state on the zeugitai, both in their military significance and as self-sufficient citizens, their economic status became progressively threatened by what can only be described as a rapacious upper class, which now consisted of both aristocrats and wealthier, non-aristocratic land owners.

These lost no opportunity of taking advantage of the frequent setbacks suffered by small farmers – crop failures, disease in livestock and so on – by imposing harsh terms for the loans that the farmers were forced to solicit, which included loss of their land or even of personal freedom – enslavement – for those who defaulted. The conditions for the landless poor, typically agricultural labourers, were even worse. These men, the *'hektemoroi'* worked for a sixth part of what they were able to produce and thus were even more vulnerable to the vicissitudes of agricultural cultivation and again to the likelihood of falling into debt, with the threat of enslavement as their bodies were their only possession.

This process, whereby the rich grew richer at the expense of the increasing population of landless and essentially workless poor, who gravitated to the city, was, by the beginning of the sixth century BC, creating a dangerous level of antagonism between the increasingly polarised classes. A level such that, as Plutarch maintains, 'there seemed to be… no other means for freeing [the city] from disturbances… to be possible but a despotic power.' In other words, Athens appeared to be ripe for a tyrannical overthrow of the state by a 'strong man' who would impose a dictatorial solution to the very clearly divided society, which was threatening to break out into *stasis* or class warfare. Such a solution was by no means without precedent in contemporary Greece, notably recently in Euboea and Mytiline. In this instance, however, the immediate response in Athens to the crisis took the form of the appointment of an individual, by a process described by Plutarch only as a choice made by the 'wisest of the Athenians' to 'succour the commonwealth and compose the differences.' This individual, Solon, refused to accept the role of a tyrant – in effect as a monarch – but insisted on assuming the constitutionally recognised position of archon specifically empowered to be 'an arbitrator and lawgiver.' Unusually, Solon came from a family made wealthy by merchandising rather than by land ownership, and was widely travelled in consequence, and was also possessed of literary ability expressed in poetry, in conformity with the exclusive convention of the time. According to Plutarch, he managed, at least initially, to find favour both with the rich because he was wealthy and with the poor because he was honest.

Solon's most dramatic act was his 'disburdening ordinance,' which became known as the *seisachtheia* or 'shaking off,' by which all outstanding debts and mortgages were cancelled (or, according to some versions, had their interest decreased). Furthermore, the demanding by lenders for debtors to pledge their bodies as security for their loans was forbidden, thus doing away with the pernicious blight of debt-slavery, and those who had been so enslaved were made free men once more. Initially, according to Plutarch (the seisachtheia), found favour with neither party, for the rich were 'angry for their money, and the poor that the land was not divided,' in other words, the land held by the rich seized and distributed amongst the landless. This general dissatisfaction gave way to a recognition of its benefits and persuaded the Athenian populace to give Solon 'entire power over everything, their magistracies, their assemblies, courts and councils.' Although the seisachtheia provided a temporary respite from debt amongst the small farmers and agricultural labourers and abolished debt-slavery, Solon did little to ease the economic plight of the hektemoroi and the others of the thetes class. He did, however, introduce reforms that fundamentally advanced their political status and, in doing so, laid the foundations of the democracy that was to be completed in the fifth century BC.

Claiming conformity with his stated intention of retaining what was good, Solon adopted the pre-existing class divisions of Athenian citizens: the *pentakosiomedimnoi*, the *hippeis*, the *zeugitai* and the thetes. Solon's innovation in this area was to recognise *thetes* as citizens, which had the result of permitting them to attend the *ekklesia* – the assembly of all male citizens. The ekklesia was not an exclusively Athenian invention but was a general feature of Greek communities, not restricted to the citizenry of city-states, but also, for example, the crews of Athenian battle fleets and other contexts in which commitment to a joint course of action was sought. Assemblies, generally, could not be described as democratic, although they clearly enabled some representation of the will of those present to be expressed, probably by the strength of acclamation rather than the casting of votes.

Ekklesiai were established sufficiently before Solon's time as to appear in both of Homer's epics. In the Iliad (2, 208-332), the Greeks, or Achaians, having experienced a combination of home-sickness and loss of faith in the support of the gods in their quest to rescue Helen, the entire force is persuaded by Odysseus to 'sweep back into the assembly place' to consider the continuation of their siege of Troy. First, they hear a diatribe from the non-aristocratic Thersites, who advise the abandonment of the campaign, followed by a personal attack, both verbal and physical, on him by Odysseus, who then successfully urges the Achaians, who 'shouted aloud' to continue their quest. Although it would be wrong to assume a close resemblance between Homer's assembly and that of Solon's era, it might be conjectured that the latter was essentially a forum where the matters under discussion were ventilated by a limited circle of speakers, probably mainly or exclusively aristocrats and the decisions were taken on the basis of acclaim, rather than voting. The role of the Thetes would almost certainly have been restricted to, at most, a vocal contribution in the form of shouts of approbation or opposition.

Solon's most radical innovation, however, was to permit the Thetes to sit on the juries that passed judgement on the probity or otherwise of the annually elected magistrates. Importantly, these juries reached their verdicts by voting, in which every citizen juror had a vote. According to Plutarch, this was thought 'nothing of' at the time, but its significance became increasingly apparent in that it placed the 'people,' amongst whom the Thetes formed an important proportion, if not a majority, in the position of holding to account magistrates, who were generally drawn from the two highest classes – one of the pre-existing arrangements that Solon had left unchanged.

Not only were the Thetes placed in this powerful position, but Solon's reforms permitted any citizen to bring an action in the courts against someone he considered to have behaved unjustly to another – not necessarily he himself. Later on, this provided Aristophanes with much comedic material arising from the legendary litigiousness of the Athenians, but as Aristotle remarked, the major democratic feature of Solon's reforms was 'what is said to have been the chief basis of the powers of the multitude, was the right of appeal to the jury-court – for the people, having the power of the vote, becomes sovereign in the government.'

While Solon's reforms went some way towards easing the lot of the zeugitai and provided the foundations of the political advancement of the lower classes, they did nothing to ameliorate the other major cause of civil strife in the Athenian state, which was the ever-simmering antagonism between the two dominant aristocrat-led clans, the 'men of the plain' and the 'men of the coast.' In fact, Solon's reforms provided a further impetus to this rivalry by being supported by the coast men under Megacles and rejected by the plain men under Lycurgus. The result of this ever-increasing rupture was the eventuality that Solon had always feared – the emergence of a strong man – a tyrant – in the person of Pisistratos, a successful general and personal friend of Solon.

Pisistratos, despite being a tyrant, a term that did not necessarily carry the modern attributes of arbitrary cruelty but simply meant someone who had assumed power unconstitutionally, according to Herodotus, 'Governed the country in an orderly and excellent manner.' Although initially professing an attachment to democracy and receiving the support of a faction of radical democrats outside the dominant clans, 'he was no revolutionary.' However, given the opportunity provided by the abandonment of their large estates by a number of the wealthiest families, including the 'accursed Alcmaeonids' (of whom later), he implemented a redistribution of their land holdings to 'those who had most need,' to whom he also provided 'start-up loans.' This action might have become a precedent, but it was never to be repeated, even at the apogee of the radical democracy of the fifth century. Apart from this undoubtedly democratic gesture, his policy was to retain the status quo 'without changing the laws or disturbing the existing magistracies,' thus his direct influence on the development of democracy was minimal, although he was responsible for laying the basis of Athenian expansion into Asia with a number of settlements in or near the Hellespont, which became highly significant to the Athenian empire and thus to the democratic regime of the later fifth century.

Pisistratos' response to the problem of the warring clans was to declare himself head of a third clan – the 'hill men' – geographically associated with the mountainous country of the North West of Attica. Although initially this resulted in a brief cessation of hostilities between the two major clans as they allied themselves against him to oust him for the first of two breaks in his rule, this reconciliation proved temporary only, but his posture of refusing to side with either while maintaining strict control over public order, backed up by mercenary troops, subdued their latent antagonism, although this remained an ever-present threat.

Following the death of Pisistratos and the subsequent genuinely oppressive reign of his son Hippias, embittered by the assassination of his fellow ruler, his brother Hipparchos, the tyranny was ended in the last decade of the sixth century BC, with Spartan assistance, by a force led by the Alcmaeonid family who had returned opportunistically from exile. Almost immediately, the 'strife of factions, led by noble and influential families, broke out,' with once again the men of the Coast and Plain, the leading antagonists. The Coast faction was headed by Kleisthenes, the head of the Alcmaeonids, who supported democracy, and his rival Isagoras, leader of the Plain Men, was in favour of oligarchy and possibly the return of the deposed tyrant Hippias. Isagoras initially gained the upper hand by being elected Archon; however, Kleisthenes managed to introduce democratic measures that were widely supported by the poor and non-citizen dispossessed, who were promised citizenship. These constituted a force large enough to intimidate Isagoras, who, in desperation, asked the Spartan King Cleomenes for assistance, having been instrumental in the revolt against the Pisistratids. Cleomenes, as a Spartan, had no sympathy for Kleisthenes' democratic ambitions and came to Athens with a small force and occupied the Acropolis. From there, he and Isagoras directed the forced exile of seven hundred families deemed to be favourable to Kleisthenes and attempted to dissolve the (relatively) democratic constitution and install an oligarchy, prefiguring the successful action of the Spartan general Lysander in 404 BC after the end of the Peloponnesian war. Cleomenes, however, was not facing an Athenian populace disheartened by defeat and starvation but one emboldened by the prospect of a new democratic regime and united against the invaders. After a brief siege, he was forced to capitulate and departed, humiliated, leaving Kleisthenes, with the returning exiles, to complete his democratic reforms.

Kleisthenes' initial objective was to end the destructive rivalry between the powerful factions based on wealthy, frequently aristocratic, land-holding families, and thus identified with specific areas of Attica. His solution to this problem was as complex as it was ingenious. It involved the creation of ten entirely artificial 'tribes,' to one of which every Athenian citizen belonged. Each tribe was geographically based, but not on a single area, rather on three separate areas, drawn from three regions: the city, the coast, and the inland. This arrangement was intended to prevent tribes falling under the control of particular factions and thus perpetuating the rivalries of the preceding century and beyond. Its contribution to the development of democracy arose from its projection into a new version of the council, or *boule*, which was changed from being a 'council of elders,' probably selected from and by the upper classes, into a representative body made up of fifty men from each tribe, elected by lot and thus guaranteed to be a mix of regional loyalties and, significantly, classes. The Boule was 'The supreme administrative body of the state,' perhaps its main function being that of a probuleutic relationship with the ekklesia, the assembly of all male citizens. This meant that no proposal could come before the ekklesia unless it had already been proposed and considered acceptable by the Boule as fit to be discussed and put to the vote there.

Kleisthenes' reforms were a very significant step towards a thoroughgoing democracy, building on Solon's initiatives. In both cases, the impulse for democratic reform came from individuals from the wealthiest class, a pattern that was to be repeated in later developments. The remaining limitations on democracy that Kleisthenes' measures left unresolved were the continuing existence of the Council of the Areopagos, consisting of ex-Archons, which in theory at least provided an oversight of the Athenian constitution, the other was the fact that, although the lower classes, the Zeugitai and the Thetes, were allowed to attend the ekklesia, and to vote, and also to sit on juries, in practice they would often not have been able to exercise these rights because of the need to earn their livings; they were also barred from the higher magistracies, including the Archonship and the treasurers. These shortcomings would have to wait for fifty years to be resolved.

Chapter 2
The Trireme and Salamis

As the title of this book implies, naval power, particularly Athenian naval power, is central to its narrative. As such, it is by no means unusual in a discussion of Greek history and culture. The Greeks, from time immemorial, have celebrated their relationship with the sea in the epics of Homer, both of which record voyages and the continuing presence of ships even in the endless years of the siege of Troy and in the heroic myths such as that of Theseus in his rescue and abandonment of Ariadne. In the Archaic period, the seventh and sixth centuries BC, sea travel became increasingly significant, both militarily, in numerous marine raids and invasions, including the establishment and support of colonies, commercially, in the transport of the burgeoning trade in goods and produce, and in a hybrid involving both of these, piracy, or privateering, for the straightforward pursuit of booty or the disabling of an enemy's trade. Given this, and in anticipation of the naval supremacy of Athens in the fifth century BC, it is surprising that the Athenians came late to the realisation of the significance of naval power, in fact, well into the fifth century BC. By contrast, a number of states had become established sea powers in the sixth century BC, of which the examples of Corinth and Samos might be instanced. Corinth, a relatively close neighbour of Athens, relied on sea traffic to support its large-scale commercial activities, assisted by its unique geographical position, which, following the construction of a causeway across the Isthmus, gave it access to both the Tyrrhenian and Aegean seas. The Corinthians found it was necessary to protect their merchant ships from piracy, for which they maintained a navy, which also became critical to their colonisation: firstly for establishing colonies, then for frequent punitive expeditions to bring rebellious ones back into line. The warships that they employed initially were galleys with fifty rowers, identified thus as *pentekonters*. These were ubiquitous in the seas surrounding Greece and probably around the Mediterranean; they were recognisably the 'fast ships' of Homer's epics, although differing from them in possessing a ram: a beak-like projection from the bows intended to damage enemy ships. Pentekonters were roomy enough to permit the carrying of provisions for the crew and thus capable of relatively long voyages within the context of the seas in which they sailed. They were also capable of carrying a number of non-rowing marines who would board enemy ships having grappled onto them. As well as being the standard warship at the beginning of the sixth century BC, they were also popular with pirates/privateers. Although fitted as standard with rams, pentekonters are not recorded as relying on ramming as a battle tactic until 540 BC, when their dominance was diminishing. A possible explanation is that a pentekonter would not have been able to reach a speed at which it could ram an enemy to inflict catastrophic damage without damage to itself; instead, the technique must have relied on a fairly slow-speed attack designed to hold the enemy followed by a disentangling manoeuvre. During the sixth century, however, a new type of warship was developed, probably by the Corinthians, which was designed to make ramming far more lethal, so much so as to make it the main function of the vessel. This type of ship, the *trireme*, was powered by essentially three pentekonter crews arranged on three levels over a hull with much the same water resistance as a single pentekonter. As such, with three times the number of rowers, the trireme was much faster. The characteristics of the trireme, as a 'fast ship,' were employed in a new form of naval warfare. Indeed it might better be described as the first kind of specifically *naval* warfare in that it replaced the old type of ship-borne fighting, which essentially utilised land-based techniques with marines armed with spears, swords and shields on ships grappled together to allow them to engage. The speed of the trireme allowed it to cripple or sink an enemy by ramming it with its bronze 'beak' or ram at or just below the water line. The technique demanded a speed approaching ten knots if the ramming vessel was not to be damaged itself, and the target ship was ideally to be hit amidships, the weakest point. In a successful ramming, the enemy ship might well be split in two. In the pursuit of the all-important speed, triremes were constructed from lighter woods than was traditional, making them prone to rot rapidly, and the size of the crew, generally reckoned to have been 200, together with its slender design, meant that there was no room for provisions. These factors made it necessary for them to be beached frequently, both to dry out and to permit the crew to purchase or steal food and wine.

The sight of a trireme with a well-trained crew at its ramming speed must have been stirring, indeed beautiful. Something of this can be seen in videos of a replica trireme, the *Olympias,* built in 1990, which are available on You Tube. The videos also give a good impression of the cramped benches occupied by the rowers, confirming the fact that the external elegance of the trireme was matched by the squalid conditions on board, particularly for the lowest bank of rowers, the *thalamioi*, who were recipients of the emanations of the two upper banks, together with the inevitable bilge water.

The potential of the trireme was not lost on other sea powers, notably Polycrates, tyrant of Samos in the sixth century BC. He had built up a force of one hundred pentekonters, with which he established a piratical sway over the island states of the Aegean, sufficiently powerful to be able to face down an attack by combined Milesian and Lesbian forces. He became aware of the probability of a more menacing threat from the Persians, whose subject Phoenicians had enthusiastically adopted the trireme, and so these state-of-the-art weapons had become available to the Great King. Polycrates recognised that his sea-going activities would have come to the notice of the Persians and that he would inevitably be confronted by a force of triremes. In consequence, he initiated a trireme construction programme, and had built up a sizeable fleet before his overthrow and execution prevented the anticipated contest.

While these developments were occurring in the late sixth century BC, the Athenians were mainly concerned with land-based activities, with the subduing of Megara and Eleusis, and the absorption of the latter into the Athenian state, and continual skirmishing on the border with Boeotia. There is little evidence of any significant marine activity other than a long-running dispute with Aegina, an island state lying across the Saronic gulf opposite Athens, whose piratical activities hampered Athenian trade, and a fairly half-hearted attempt to support the rebellion of the Ionian Greeks against Persia in 495 BC, for which a number of ships, almost certainly pentekonters, went to the Eastern Aegean. The war against Aegina was a matter of coastal raids, for which again pentekonters were used, and no sea battles as such took place, and the Athenian support for the Ionians had disappeared by the time of the battle at Lade, for which the Ionians had assembled a force of triremes under the Phocaean Dionysus but were defeated by their Persian counterparts. It is clear that the Athenians were capable of assembling forces of pentekonters, but exactly how these were provided is a matter of conjecture. The Athenian constitution of the time included geographically defined entities named *naucraries*, which term has frequently been interpreted as 'ship boards,' normally by scholars who have accepted the opinion of an ancient commentator writing some seven centuries afterward that each *naucrari* was responsible for providing a ship for the service of the state, and may thus be seen as the forerunner of the *trierarchic* system that was later established for the upkeep of the navy. Others have suggested that this view depends on an erroneous assumption that the *nau* prefix indicates a naval connection, as in *naus*, Greek for ship, and have maintained that the term was simply applied to a region identified for purposes of taxation. This is how Aristotle in the *Athenian Constitution* (viii, 3) appears to use it. It is possible that wealthy aristocrats may have owned and operated penetekonters, possibly for privateering, and made them available to the state for warfare in much the same way that they would make their horses available for land-based conflicts.

The sources (Herodotus, Aristotle, and Plutarch) present the Athenian adoption of the trireme as a sudden transformation brought about by Themistocles almost on the eve of the naval battle of Salamis, at which Greek, mainly Athenian, forces confronted the fleet of the Persian king Xerxes during his invasion of Greece. It is certainly the case that the moving spirit behind the adoption of the trireme and a corresponding change of focus of Athenian strategy from land warfare to marine was Themistocles, who was Archon in the four-nineties and was a powerful influence in the Assembly. He had become convinced that Athens' destiny lay in becoming a maritime power and thus of the necessity of building and manning a correspondingly powerful navy equipped with the trireme – currently the most formidable naval weapon. However, Themistocles' success in persuading the Athenians to adopt a maritime strategy based on the trireme was not universally popular at the time and was opposed particularly by another leading politician, Aristides. His objection was based essentially on the recognition that the creation of a large navy would inevitably bring the *thetes*, the lowest class of citizen, from which the crews of the triremes would be largely drawn, into the role of front-line defenders of the city. In this, they would replace the hoplite classes, inevitably reinforcing the development of radical democracy, a development to which he was strongly opposed. Aristides was ostracised, however, and Themistocles' plans went ahead, with the result, as Plutarch wrote, with anachronistic exaggeration (*Life of Themistocles*, 19), 'He increased the standing of the people at the upper class's expense and filled them full of confidence, with power now passing into the hands of sailors, boatswains and pilots.'

Plutarch's apothegm was thirty years ahead of its time, but it captures the perceived connexion that was well established in Themistocles' time between the development of the navy and democracy.

The initial spur to the adoption of the trireme was an increase in the intensity of the conflict with Aegina in response to which the Athenians had purchased twenty triremes from Corinth, which was favourably disposed towards Athens at the time, at the knock-down price of five drachmai each. This piece of good fortune was then outshone by the Athenians' discovery of two silver mines at Laurium, some of the proceeds from which were used to build 200 triremes. The sources vary in their description of the management of this activity. Herodotus (7.144) says merely that Themistocles persuaded the Athenians, rather than distributing the proceeds from the mines (presumably the initial yield) to the entire male citizenship at the rate of ten drachmai each, to build the triremes. (Plutarch/Aristotle) provides a different version in which the silver bounty was distributed to wealthy individuals at the rate of one Talent each, with the proviso that they should use the money each to finance the building of a trireme. This version presages in some respects the arrangement by which the Athenian fleet was maintained and augmented in the years following Salamis when it became the main and indispensable military arm of the Athenian state. This arrangement depended on a partnership between the state, which underwrote the actual construction of the ships, and a group of extremely wealthy individuals, the *trierarchs*, who assumed financial responsibility for at least part of their fitting out and running costs: each ship, at least for most of the fifth century, being the responsibility of one trierarch for one year. The institution of the trierarchy was one, probably the most financially onerous, of the *liturgies*, which were established as 'conduits for the transfer of wealth from the rich to the people.' Its detailed operation, which is dealt with later, is both interesting and relevant to this book in that it provided a generally successful relationship between democracy and the wealthiest Athenian citizens. Salamis actually provided the last known instance of a privately owned warship, a trireme with a crew of two hundred which was financed entirely by its owner and commander Cleinias, son of Alcibiades (Herodotus 8, 17), who must have been outstandingly wealthy. Cleinias' son, also an Alcibiades, was a character who achieved great fame, not to say notoriety, in the latter part of the Peloponnesian war and appears frequently in the relevant parts of this book.

The notion that the two-hundred-strong fleet of triremes sprang into fully operational existence almost overnight is, to say the least, questionable. The infrastructure and skilled manpower needed for their construction must have taken some time to assemble and may very well have relied on foreign expertise and labour, probably from the Corinthians. Then there is the question of the crews. The standard complement of a trireme, according to various sources, was 200, of which 170 were rowers, sixteen were ships' officers and deck hands, with ten marines and four archers. Of these, only the armed deck party would have been recruited straightforwardly from land-based hoplites and archers; the rest would have required extensive training, particularly the *kybernautai*, or helmsmen, whose expertise was vital to the navigation of the ships, particularly in the battle environment. This training could have been undertaken only on the triremes themselves and might reasonably be assumed to have been carried out in an incremental way in a rolling programme as the ships came into service. The question of the manning of the Athenian fleet is a complex one, which is considered later in this book. Suffice it to say that the *Decree of Themistocles*, a somewhat disputed epigraphic source, specifies that the crews of the Athenian ships at

Salamis were either Athenian citizens or foreigners living in Athens.

The sea battle in 471 BC off the island of Salamis, which lies opposite the coastal area of Athens, came to possess an iconic status for the Greeks generally, and the Athenians particularly, in much the same sort of way that the English defeat of the Spanish Armada had for England. Both cases saw the prevention of the overthrow of a nascent democratic regime by a despotic absolute monarchy, specifically in the case of Salamis, laying the basis for the frustration and ultimate defeat of the invasion of Greece by Xerxes, the 'Great King' of Persia. The Athenians, against whom the Persian king nursed a particular animus, both for their role in the defeat of the previous Persian invasion at the battle of Marathon and their democratic tendencies, played a major role in the battle under their commander, the proponent of naval power, Themistocles.

Xerxes' had assembled a colossal invasion force consisting of a land army of something over two million, including auxiliaries and camp servants, and a fleet of over a thousand ships. Having crossed the Hellespont over a bridge of tethered ships, the army marched around the Aegean, creating destitution and famine as it went as the inhabitants of the locales through which it progressed were obliged to supply its gargantuan requirement for food. At the same time, the fleet sailed around the coast, maintaining contact with the army and imposing its own demand for rations. As the force approached their territory, the Greeks, some of them, for once, were able to forget, at least temporarily, their differences in attempting to devise resistance to this overwhelming threat. As part of these preparations, a fleet was assembled, in which the Athenians were numerically most significant, providing 180 triremes. The fleet was under the overall command of a Spartan, Eurybiadas, as the result of the recognition of Sparta's pre-eminence in land warfare and despite her limited experience of naval fighting – an indication of the prevailing attitudes towards the relative importance of the two theatres.

Xerxes' land army, having defeated Greek forces at Thermopylae, including the famous 'three hundred' Spartans under their King Leonidas, moved rapidly through Boeotia with the assistance of the pro-Persian Thebans and were clearly about to invade the city of Athens. After something approaching panic seized the Athenian military leaders, the Council of the Areopagos took the decisive step of commanding an evacuation of the city to the island of Salamis, which faced the coastal area of Athens, adding as inducement a payment of eight drachmai to each citizen who agreed to go. The evacuation duly took place using the ships of the combined Greek fleet, which had assembled off Athens, and the city was left almost deserted, save for, depending on which version of events is accepted, a few 'poor people and priests,' or a small rear guard, in either case on the Acropolis. When Xerxes' forces invested in the city, the defenders of the Acropolis held them off for a short time but were eventually overwhelmed, and the temple of Athene, the titular goddess of Athens, was burnt.

As Xerxes' land army was progressing south, it was tracked down the Aegean coast by his fleet, which, on the way, suffered considerable losses – over four hundred ships, according to Herodotus – in a violent storm off Thessaly. On the same day as the beginning of the battle at Thermopylae, the Persian fleet came in sight of the Greek fleet, which had sailed out of the Saronic Gulf and north around Euboea, a large island off the Aegean coast and had reached Artemision on its north-east coast. The commanders of the Greek fleet, who included the Peloponnesians and the Spartan Eurybiadas, were mainly for retreating back to the Gulf, having been disconcerted by the size of the enemy force. The inhabitants of Euboea, having been convinced that they would be defended by the Greek fleet against the Persians, were thrown into a state of panic on learning of this and rapidly raised a considerable sum of money, thirty Talents, to persuade the fleet to stay and fight. The money was given to Themistocles, the commander of the Athenian contingent, who prevailed upon Eurybiadas to commit to confronting the Persian fleet by means of bribing him with six Talents, Themistocles pocketing the rest. The Greeks then attacked the Persians, who appeared to be taken aback initially and offered little resistance, losing a number of ships before the encounter was broken off at nightfall. On the next day, the Persians were determined to seize the initiative and attack the Greeks. Having been assured by a captured Greek that the Greek fleet was about to retreat through the narrow and rocky channel between Euboea and the Attic mainland, they sent two hundred ships south around the east coast of the island with the intention of rounding its southernmost point and then sailing north to trap the reputedly retreating Greek fleet. Once again, the weather took a hand, and a storm drove many of the Persian ships onto the rocks as they attempted to navigate the channel.

Meanwhile, the Persians' main force engaged the Greeks, who adopted a classic defence tactic where their ships manoeuvring them together stern first, with their bows pointing radially outwards. This was only partially successful, however, and both sides suffered significant losses before they retreated to their respective anchorages. Despite having accepted the money from the Euboeans, on the next day, the Greek fleet sailed south down the coastal channel unimpeded by any Persian ships. They then sailed into the Saronic Gulf with the intention of reaching the Isthmus near Corinth, where some of their number, particularly the Peloponnesians, thought it would be best to face the Persian fleet for a decisive confrontation. Their choice of this location was based on the closeness of their land troops, particularly the Spartans, perhaps reflecting a lack of confidence in the effectiveness of their naval forces. In the event, however, they anchored off Salamis, while the Persian fleet was not far behind, anchoring in the bay of Phaleron to the east of the Piraeus, the coastal settlement of Athens.

The site of the subsequent battle, the geography of which was highly significant to its unfolding, was the narrow strait between the Attic shore and the island of Salamis. The strait extends north-west from the Bay of Phaleron, where the Persian fleet was anchored, and then bends to the west around the long promontory, Cynosura, that points east from Salamis. The Greek fleet was anchored on the north side of this promontory, which was effectively extended by a small island known at the time as Psyttalaeia, which lies to the south of the eastern tip of the promontory and between it and the Attic coast, thus forming a 'choke point' obliging an attacking fleet from the south to divide around it.

The commanders of the Greek fleet met in continuous session on the evening before the battle. Initially, they had decided to follow their original plan to sail north further up the Saronic Gulf to reach more open waters near the Isthmus. Themistocles, however, was convinced that the best hope for victory was to give battle in the restricted waters between Salamis and the Attic coast, where the numerical superiority of the Persian fleet would work to its own disadvantage. Whether consciously or not, this is strikingly similar to the choice of Thermopylae, where constraining the numerically superior enemy to a narrow defile enabled a comparatively small force to inflict heavy casualties. Themistocles' plan was to wait for the Persian fleet to attack northwards and then to attack its left wing as it emerged past the west side of Psyttalaeia, then to engage the right wing as it rounded the island from the east, very probably losing its formation as it did so. This plan was under consideration by the commanders of the fleet but was increasingly coming under opposition, particularly from the Peloponnesians, including Eurybiadas, who had been overawed by the size of the Persian fleet and also disturbed by the reports that the

Persians had landed a sizeable force of infantry on Psyttaleia, in anticipation of a battle around the island with the intention of saving wrecked Persian and allied crews and killing similarly affected Greek sailors. They wished to revert to the original plan to make a stand near the Isthmus and proposed, therefore, that the Greek fleet should sail north around Salamis. This, of course, went against Themistocles belief that the only way to defeat the Persians was to fight them in the straits. In order to carry the meeting, he resorted to subterfuge, sending a slave named Sicinnus, who spoke Persian, to the Persian camp at Piraeus to tell the Persian leaders, in a message from Themistocles proclaiming his support for Xerxes, that the Greeks were demoralised and intended to sail away in the night and that if the Persians attacked the Greeks at Salamis, the Athenians would turn against their allies and victory would be theirs. The Persians believed this story and immediately despatched two hundred ships to sail around the west coast of Salamis to block any attempt at escape via the northern route, while the south was blocked anyway. Having thus bottled up the Greek fleet, Xerxes decided to delay the attack until dawn. The stage was set, therefore, for the battle to take place, as Themistocles had planned, in the strait. It might be pointed out also that, should the victory go to the Persians, Themistocles' ruse would provide him with a claim on them, probably guaranteeing him at least survival and possibly acceptance by the victors.

In a new development, Aristides, Themistocles' political enemy who had been ostracised but then recalled in response to the threat of invasion, had returned in a ship from Aegina and arrived at the Council of war at the Greek fleet after considerable difficulty in avoiding the Persian ships which were 'everywhere.' He met Themistocles outside the meeting and told him that the Greeks were surrounded and would have to fight in the straits of Salamis. This, of course, was exactly the outcome that Themistocles' trick was intended to produce and having agreed with Aristides that their previous mutual antipathy should be forgotten, he sent him into the meeting to apprise the commanders of the situation. They, however, were unwilling to believe the news and were persuaded only by the arrival of a ship deserting from the Persians, the crew of which provided confirmation.

Unusually for battles in the fifth century BC, or indeed very many historic battles, we actually have what is effectively an eye-witness account by the tragedian Aeschylos, who was certainly present there and is reliably recorded as having fought with the Greek fleet. His account is incorporated in his tragedy *Persai* (the Persians), which was performed in public some eight years after the battle. Whilst his account was doubtless written for dramatic effect rather than historical accuracy, it is difficult to believe that its salient features contained important distortions; his audience would have contained men who had also fought in the battle and would have reacted to gross inaccuracies. Despite this contemporary evidence, the battle has engendered considerable subsequent conflict, albeit less lethal than the original but robust nevertheless, between the academic proponents of differing versions of its course. What follows, together with the description of the events leading up to the battle given above, is an attempt to characterise the generally accepted version, although there will inevitably be dissension.

As dawn broke on the next day, the Persian fleet sailed northwards from Phaleron, formed in a crescent comprised of three lines of ships, with the arms of the crescent leading the centre. On the right wing, nearest the Attic coast were the Ionian Greeks, who were forced to fight for Xerxes as his subjects. On the left were the Phoenicians, who passed to the East of Psyttaleia. At about the same time, the Greeks, having been harangued by Themistocles, embarked and sailed out to form their line of battle, with the Peloponnesians on the right wing and the Athenians on the left, off the point of Cynosura. As they were manoeuvring into place, the Greeks sang in united defiance, being heard by the approaching Persian fleet, who were surprised and demoralised, having been led to believe that the Greeks were attempting to flee in disorder. By the time that the Greeks had formed their line, the Persians were almost upon them. After a brief hesitation, a Greek ship commanded by Ameinias rammed one of the enemies, who turned out to be Phoenician and became entangled with it. This spurred the Athenian ships to go to the assistance of their comrade and rapidly to mount a general attack that spread across the whole extent of the Persians' front rank. Within a short time, Themistocles' prognostication was being realised, as the Persian ships attempted either to attack the Greeks or to escape from them in the restricted space, collapsing their formation into a confused melee in which many collided with lethal effect with ships being damaged and sunk, and banks of oars smashed.

Meanwhile, the Greeks circled round, picking off their victims as they became sufficiently isolated. Something of the disorder and panic of the Persian fleet is conveyed by the incident involving Artemisia, Queen of Halicarnassos, that forms nearly all of Herodotus' description of the actual battle. In this incident, the trireme (uniquely) captained by a woman, Artemisia, Queen of Hallicarnassos, then under Persian control and thus fighting with the Persian fleet, in her panic to flee from a pursuing Athenian trireme rammed an allied ship that happened to be in the way and sank it with all hands. The Athenian captain broke off his pursuit, thinking that her ship must be an ally, and was mortified to discover his mistake as a prize of 10,000 drachmai had been put on Artemisia's head by the Athenians, who were offended at being challenged by a woman. (Herodotus was born in Hallicarnassos, which may explain the prominence he gives to the incident.) As the confusion developed into a rout, the survivors of the Persian fleet fled back to the bay of Phaleron and anchored for the night. Having witnessed the crushing defeat of his navy from a mountain overlooking the strait, Xerxes was clearly shocked, and despite announcing plans to build a defensive wall of ships to protect what remained, was unable to hide his desire from his cousin Mardonius to return to Persia, afraid that the victorious Greeks might attack his boat bridge over the

Hellespont. Sensing this, Mardonius proposed that the Xerxes should return immediately while leaving himself with 300,000 picked troops to continue the campaign. After some discussion with his advisors, including the redoubtable Artemisia, who had counselled against the battle at Salamis, and who now agreed with Mardonius' proposal, his plan was accepted. The main part of Xerxes' army then began their march back around the Aegean, while his navy, which the Greeks had been expecting to return to the fray, slipped quietly away.

On the discovery of the departure of the Persian fleet, the Greek commanders set out to pursue the dispersing enemy but were unable to overtake them, and they stopped at the island of Andros to consider their options. There was considerable support for an attack on the bridge of ships across the Hellespont, with a view to hindering Xerxes' eventual retreat to Persia. Themistocles persuaded his fellow commanders against this idea, probably on the grounds of the dangers of the Greek ships being caught out by Persian forces having regained some spirit as they neared their home bases. In fact, his private reason for apparently failing to press home such an advantageous position was more concerned with his instinct for self-preservation. He sent a message carried by the ubiquitous Sicinnus to Xerxes, claiming that he had saved the king from further disasters by holding back the triumphant Greek fleet. Themistocles appears to the modern eye at least a deeply 'complex' character: without doubt, he was the architect of the victory at Salamis, both with his long-term strategic obsession with changing Athens into a dominant maritime power, and his tactical brilliance in choosing the site of the confrontation with the Persian fleet. And yet his double-edged ruse to persuade the Persians to attack at Salamis while also providing him personally with insurance against a Persian victory, together with this attempt to place an obligation on Xerxes, should it become necessary, seems to reflect something approaching treachery. Eventually, this desire to play for both sides would catch up with him.

The connexion between the navy and democracy inspired most ancient commentators, particularly Aristotle, who were antipathetic to democracy, to downplay the significance of the battle of Salamis. Instead, they emphasised the land battles of Thermopylae and Plataea, where the heroes were the heavy-armed hoplites in Athens, drawn mainly from the zeugitai and knights – the traditional custodians of military prowess. It is true that after Salamis, a sizeable portion of his army remained in Greece under the command of his cousin Mardonius, with the intention of attacking the Peloponnese in the next year. This attack, which duly took place, was defeated at Plataea by a combined Greek force led by the Spartans under their general Pausanias, finally terminating the Persian invasion. It is the case, however, that Xerxes had departed with the main part of the army on their long and beleaguered retreat through Thessaly, Macedonia and Thrace almost immediately after the defeat of his fleet, having been unnerved by the naval disaster. Without Salamis, it is likely that the Persians would have overrun the whole of Greece. However, at the time, it was largely left to the playwrights, particularly Aeschylus and Aristophanes, to celebrate the crucial role of the Greek, particularly Athenian, naval force in Xerxes' defeat.

On the same day as the battle of Plataea, a Greek fleet, largely consisting of Athenian forces but led by the Spartan Leotychides, discovered and attacked the remnants of Xerxes' navy. The demoralised commanders had been apprised of the Greeks' approach and had beached their ships close to Persian land forces at Mycale on the Ionian (modern Turkish) coast, hoping by this to avoid a sea battle and get help from their land-based allies. The Greeks also beached their ships and disembarked troops, which suggests that at least part of their force comprised transports, which were also triremes but equipped for troop-carrying rather than speed. The subsequent engagement, which largely involved Athenian soldiers, was hard-fought but ended in a Greek victory. The Persian ships were burnt, and most of their crews were 'cut to pieces' in Herodotus' words (9, 114).

With the destruction of Xerxes' forces, both land and maritime, the Athenians were able to return to their city, which lay in ruins after occupation first by Xerxes and then Mardonius. Under Themistocles' direction, they first concentrated on rebuilding the walls of the city and then, at his further insistence, undertook the construction of three fortified harbours at the Piraeus so that the victorious fleet should have a permanent and secure base.

Chapter 3
The Delian League and the Athenian Empire

After the defeat of the Persian invasion of the mainland, the Greeks turned their attention to the Persian rule over the 'Ionian' Greek settlements on the islands and east coast of the Aegean. Pausanias, the Spartan victor of the battle of Plataea, at which the remnants of Xerxes' army still in Greece had been defeated, was sent in command of an allied Hellenic expeditionary force, including twenty ships from Peloponnesus and thirty from Athens, to free the Ionian Greeks from Persian domination. The force began their campaign at Cyprus, where they 'subdued the greater part' (Thuc 1, 94), then took control of Byzantium, at the Black Sea end of the Propontis, from the Persians.

Pausanias had already offended his own Spartan colleagues by his action immediately after Plataea in inscribing a boastful message celebrating the victory as his personal triumph on the memorial erected at Delphi after the battle. He then began to display megalomaniac tendencies, treating his supposed allies with arrogance and a violent temper. These particularly offended the Ionian Greeks, notably those who had been freed from Persian rule and were loath to submit to another tyranny, moreover, one imposed by, supposedly, a fellow Greek. In consequence, the Ionian Greeks demanded that Athens should assume the leadership of the anti-Persian force and also protect them against the increasingly oppressive Pausanias. The Ionians were, in many cases, descended from Athenian colonists, and Athens frequently claimed, despite her location on the Greek mainland, to be an Ionian city and to possess a parental relationship to them. It was perhaps not surprising that Pausanias' behaviour aside, they should prefer Athenian to Spartan leadership.

The ephors, the powerful magistrates of Sparta who could overrule a king, on hearing of Pausanias' behaviour, recalled him to face accusations, including treasonous communications with the Persian king. After a bizarre sequence of defiant episodes, Pausanias was eventually condemned to death. He sought sanctuary in the Temple of Athena in Sparta, where, being inviolable, his fellow citizens walled him up, and he died of starvation, thereby defiling the temple, an incident that would come back to haunt the Spartans. In his place, the Spartan authorities sent Dorcis with a small force, but the Ionians refused to accept his leadership, and he returned home. The Spartans then washed their hands of the whole enterprise, leaving the field open to the Athenians. Again, this was not surprising as they had been traditionally reluctant to pursue operations outside mainland Greece, being content, as they saw it, with their leadership there.

This led to the formation, under Athenian leadership, of the Delian confederacy, or league, of city-states around the Aegean coast and on the islands, with the intention both of providing an alliance against Persia and of obtaining reparations to compensate for the oppression of Persian rule in Ionia and the proximate islands and the invasion of Greece. This was to be done by the eviction of Persian forces with the consequent seizure of both goods and personnel, who could be ransomed or sold into slavery. The league was named after the island of Delos, the mythical birthplace of the immortal twins Apollo and Artemis, which was sacred to the Ionian Greeks and also to the Athenians, in keeping with their Ionian patronage. Peisistratos had 'sanctified' the island by removing mortal graves from the locality of a shrine of Apollo. On a more mundane level, the treasury of the league was held there, and the regular meetings of representatives of the members of the league were held there under the leadership of the Athenians.

The fact that the creation and siting of the treasury were coincidental with the inception of the league was indicative of the manner by which Athens exercised its leadership. The alliance was to be essentially a maritime one, and the members were required either to provide ships for combined operations under an Athenian commander-in-chief or, if they could not or preferred not to engage in naval warfare, to provide money which Athens would use to maintain her navy to a level consistent with the objectives of the league. Before being transmitted to the Delian treasury, this money was to be brought to Athens on an annual basis to an office specially set up for the purpose that of the *Hellenotamiai*, or Hellenic Treasurers. These payments were referred to as *phoros*, a term normally used to mean tribute paid by a subject people to a superior power. The amount of the phoros paid by those members from whom it was due was initially specified by Aristides and totalled 460 Talents. (Aristides had overcome his aversion to naval forces and was an enthusiastic supporter of the league and, particularly, Athens' leadership of it. In this, he had effectively replaced his old rival Themistocles, who had been implicated with Pausanias in treasonous dealings with the Persian king and had been forced to flee, finally ending up as governor of a Persian province granted to him by the king – an astonishing demarche for the architect of Xerxes' defeat at Salamis, although perhaps confirming the success of his claiming to have saved Xerxes from an even greater disaster by persuading his fellow commanders to leave the king's boat bridge over the Hellespont untouched.)

Whether by design or not, the effect of the constitution of the league was to increase rapidly the size of the Athenian navy. As Thucydides remarks, 'For the majority of them [the allies] disliked military service and absence from home, and so they agreed to contribute their share of the expense instead of ships.' After a time, only Samos, Chios and Lesbos maintained their own fleets and made them available for the common defence. 'Whereby the Athenian navy was proportionately increased.' The resulting dominance of the Athenian navy in the Aegean and the eastern Mediterranean was not a glamour project but was of comprehensive importance to the state in maintaining its control over the league and pursuing its strategic goals, initially against Persia and, later, Sparta. The availability of 'fast ships' – invariably triremes – able to project Athenian power at virtually any point in the Aegean within a day or two was essential, as, of course, was the availability of trained crews to man them.

The first Athenian commander in chief of the league was Kimon, son of Miltiades, who had been involved in colonial and commercial interests in the area around the estuary of the river Strymon in Thrace (modern Turkey). In conducting his campaign against the Persian king's forces and land holdings, Kimon certainly achieved a sequence of victories consistent with its objectives – the roll-back of the 'barbarians' – but also found time to extend Athens' influence for commercial gain, not always in a manner respecting the interests of his allies. One example of this was his following his father's example at the Strymon estuary. This area was also subject of considerable interest to the closely located island of Thasos, a member of the league, and which became increasingly unwilling to accept Athenian incursion in what it considered to be its own backyard, which moreover possessed valuable mining assets.

These conflicting commercial interests were not the only cause of the uneasy relationship between Athens and her allies, which rapidly developed within a short time from the inception of the league. Something of the flavour of this can be gleaned from the oath of allegiance sworn by new members of the league, which both emphasised their commitment to the *plethos* – the common people of Athens – and acknowledged Athens' preeminent role in the clause, 'I will not desert the plethos of Athens, nor the allies of the Athenians.' Parenthetically, the oath is also highly significant in its identification of the supreme authority of the Athenian state as the plethos, confirming its democratic nature to its allies. This was before the introduction of the 'radical democracy' that was to be established later in the development of the league. The oath also makes very clear that defection from the league, or 'desertion of the plethos of Athen,' was to be regarded as an extremely serious matter from almost the beginning of the league, tantamount to a revolt against Athenian leadership, even though the fiction of 'first amongst equals' was still half-heartedly maintained. The determination and collection of the phoros were also a constant source of friction. Thucydides writes, 'Now while there were other causes of revolts, the principal ones were the failures in bringing in the tribute or their quota of ships and, in some cases, refusal of military service; for the Athenians exacted the tribute strictly and gave offence by applying coercive measures to any who were unaccustomed or unwilling to bear the hardships of service.'

The first major revolt, or attempted desertion, was that of Naxos in 466 BC, which was attacked by the Athenian fleet and reduced 'by blockade.' Thucydides adds the portentous comment that 'this was the first of the allied cities which were enslaved contrary to Hellenic right; the turn of the others came later.' Naxos then became a 'subject state' under the direct rule of Athens. The same fate befell Carystos, a city at the south end of the island of Euboea, off the east coast of Attica and close to Athens, and somewhat distant from any Persian influence. The

Carystians had resisted membership of the league, much to the Athenians' displeasure, and so they were forced into subject status by military action. The Island of Thasos, as remarked previously, was unhappy with Athenian incursions into the Thracian littoral and also revolted against them. The resulting conflict lasted several years and, at one point, threatened to develop into a war between Athens and Sparta, as the Thasians urged the Spartans to come to their aid. The Spartans were about to set out when they were distracted by the Helot revolt that was eventually to involve Kimon. The Thasians then sued for peace and were forced to give up their ships, pull down their walls, and pay both an immediate indemnity and an annual tribute. This pattern of 'allies' tiring of Athenian hegemony and being subjected to generally increasingly harsh measures to force them back into an unwilling servitude continued well into the second Peloponnesian war, with, as Cawkwell remarks, the Athenian fleet acting as the police force of what was now developing all the characteristics of an empire.

It is, of course, not the case that the Athenian forces were entirely occupied with keeping their allies and subject states in line. In 465 BC (probably), an allied force led by Kimon inflicted a crushing defeat on both land and sea on Persian forces at the river Eurymedon in Pamphylia (on the modern Turkish coast). This effectively ended Persian influence in the Aegean and the coast of Asia Minor for half a century. It might have been thought that Eurymedon rendered the Delian League, formed to confront Persian oppression, redundant, a sentiment probably espoused by many of the league's members. The Athenians, however, had become habituated to their hegemony and had no wish to see their ambitions curtailed nor to dispense with the financial support that accrued from it. This reluctance to let go of the league was intensified by the increasingly hostile relations with Sparta. These had been dramatically worsened by the clumsy behaviour of the Spartans, who had requested Athenian assistance in confronting the revolt of the Helots, the slave underclass that the Spartans maintained in a state of enforced suppression, but when Kimon brought five thousand hoplites to the siege of the rebel forces at Ithumi, the Spartans got cold feet at the dash and esprit of the Athenians, and in Thucydides' words, 'Smote Athens in the face' telling them that their help was not required. Not unnaturally, the Athenian populace, who had been largely against Kimon's expedition, took this as a gross insult. Relations continued to worsen as the Athenians became less concerned with Ionia and less accepting of Sparta's hegemony on the mainland. Given this, the Athenians were not so much reluctant, as incapable, of releasing their allies, as they pivoted their strategic focus away from Persia and against Sparta.

As part of this new interest in mainland Greece, the Athenians took the side of Megara in a dispute with Corinth. Despite both being close neighbours of Athens, they were regarded as Peloponnesian states and thus subject to Spartan influence. However, Sparta had supported Corinth, and the Megarians revolted against them, and the Athenians took the opportunity of signing them up as an ally. In this, they went as far as assisting the Megarians to fortify their city and built long walls from it to the port of Nisaea and also provided a permanent garrison there. This episode prompted a hatred of the Athenians on the part of the Corinthians, which was to grow and to last at least until the end of the century. This also further increased the Spartans' antipathy to Athens following the debacle at Ithumi. The two were at war by 458 BC.

At about the same time, the son of the Libyan king, Inaros, had fomented a revolt in Egypt against the rule of the Persian king Artaxerxes there and urged the Athenians to assist him in taking over the country. The Athenians had recently sent a force of two hundred ships on an expedition to Cyprus, and this was diverted to Egypt, apparently with little forethought as to the advisability of opening a new theatre of war, particularly with the old and powerful Persian foe. Initially, all went well. The Athenian fleet sailed into the Nile and made themselves 'masters of the river and two-thirds of Memphis,' and there, effectively, they stayed while making little headway towards further conquest. Eventually, after a failed attempt by the Persians to involve the Spartans, a Persian general, Megabyzes, was sent with a large army, and the revolt was extinguished and the Athenian force defeated, losing not only the ships it arrived in but also most of a relief force of fifty triremes which, in ignorance of the latest developments, had sailed into the Nile and been attacked. This was the first real disaster of the democratic regime in Athens.

Rather surprisingly, the building of the Megarian walls predated by four years the Athenians' construction of their own 'long walls,' which connected the city of Athens to the Piraeus and the bay of Phaleron, which adjoined the east of the Piraeus, essentially creating an 'island' that was well-protected from the land and provided an equally well-defended access to the sea so that the city could never be starved into submission, provided the navy retained its superiority.

During the building of the Long Walls towards the end of 457 BC, a Spartan-led force of Peloponnesians entered Boeotia, north of Attica, where they prevented an invasion of Dorian territory by the Phocians. While they were still present in Boeotia, they had received representations from disenchanted Athenian oligarchs, requesting that they put an end to the democracy and prevent the completion of the Long Walls – always seen as a provocation by both the anti-democratic faction and, indeed, the Spartans themselves. The Athenian authorities were well aware of these machinations and determined to nip the threat in the bud, sending their entire land force with some allied contingents into Boeotia to confront the Peloponnesian force. In the resulting battle at Tanagra, 'after great slaughter on both sides,' the Peloponnesians were victorious; however, they did not press on into Athens but returned to Peloponnesus via Megara, where they inflicted some damage. A couple of months later, the Athenians made another expedition into Boeotia, where they defeated the Boeotians at Oenophyta 'and became masters of Boeotia and Phocis.' They then completed the

Long Walls, and soon afterward, the Aeginetans, with whom the Athenians had been conducting yet another campaign, agreed to terms, dismantled their walls, gave up their ships and agreed to pay the *phoros*.

At this juncture, it had become clear that the Delian League had morphed into an Athenian *thalassocracy* – a maritime empire in which its 'allies' and 'subject states' were effectively controlled by the Athenian democratic regime, not only for matters of foreign policy and defence but reaching down to quite low-level administrative matters. Academic opinion with respect to this transformation varies between that of a dramatic sea-change at some time, possibly after Eurymedon, and an alternative that sees Athens as having intended from its inception that the league should form the basis of Athenian hegemony. Of these two poles, the second is perhaps nearer the truth in that the Athenians' interpretation of the original objectives of the league and the harshness of the treatment of 'desertion' was simply inconsistent with the idea of a loose defence federation. An event that provided at least a strong symbolic indication of the transformation of the Delian League into the Athenian empire took place in 454 BC when the Athenians decided to re-site the treasury of the league at the Athenian Acropolis. Whilst it is true that the significance of the location at Delos was largely symbolic – the payment of the *Phoros* into the treasury was handled by the *Helenotamiai* when they had received it in Athens after all – it was a further indication that any idea of the league as a confederation of equals conjoined by ties of ancestry and the worship of the Delian

Apollo had been overtaken by one informed simply by the overwhelming power of Athens, with the appropriate religious oversight being switched to Athene.

In addition to the imposition of the *phoros* and the occasional demands for military support, Athenian hegemony developed in a number of imperialistic directions, involving both the subject states and the 'autonomous' allies. These were required to adopt Athenian coinage, based on the Athenian silver drachma and weights and measures. These were probably beneficial, and in the main welcomed, in encouraging trade throughout the Aegean region, which also benefitted from the suppression of piracy by the Athenian navy. Other measures were much less popular, including the requirement for all legal cases, both civil and criminal, above a certain degree of seriousness, to be heard in an Athenian law court: normally one of the *heliaea*, the people's courts, or in the case of murder, that of the Council of the Areopagos. This necessitated considerable expenditure on the part of the litigants in travelling to Athens and staying there until their case was brought forward. It was also seen as a humiliation on the part of the subject states and allies, particularly in having their sovereignty over justice removed. It was also the case that the *heliaea*, in which the jurors were largely drawn from the *plethos,* were notoriously unsympathetic to litigants displaying oligarchic or plutocratic tendencies, and could not be necessarily relied upon to bring in the 'correct' verdict.

The law courts also came into play in the political control of the empire. The Athenians were well aware that their hegemony was not universally popular throughout its extent. Indeed, they were told by both Pericles, the figurehead of the democracy, and by the demagogue Cleon, held up as his antithesis by both Thucydides and Aristophanes, that their empire was a tyranny. Consequently, they had created an intelligence service that was capable of detecting potential trouble in the form of anti-Athenian feelings at an early stage. The basis of this service was the *proxenoi* and *archontes,* who were based in each of the empire states, together with travelling inspectors. The institution of *proxenoi* was widespread in Greece and took the form of citizens of foreign states who had some connection to another, such as Athens, and who represented that state in their own. It was conventional for each *proxenos* to be guaranteed safety by treaty between the states involved. Part of the role of a *proxenos* was to supply information as to political developments in his state to the associated state. *Archontes* were Athenian citizens who were stationed more-or-less permanently in league states to keep an eye on them. There were also the hated sycophants, or informers, and the cleruchs, who were Athenian citizens given land in the states and who acted as an informal garrison. All these agents of the Athenian state were constantly on the lookout for individuals who could be accused of 'stirring up revolt against Athens,' resulting in a writ and a summons to face a charge in the Athenian court, often apparently on fairly flimsy grounds. (Aristophanes provides a satirical account of an informer in *Birds* 1422-32.) The sight of an Athenian trireme newly arrived in harbour must have been unsettling, to say the least, for someone who had been less than circumspect in his criticism of Athenian dominance. The subsequent enforced journey to Athens can hardly have been pleasant, with the additional aspect that some of the rowers propelling the ship might be amongst the jury who would pass judgement on him.

The period from the mid-century down to 432 BC, which saw the start of the Peloponnesian war, might well be regarded as the apogee of the Athenian empire, during which Athens increased her wealth to the benefit of virtually all her citizens and generally consolidated her power. The treasury in the Acropolis had developed a considerable and growing surplus occasioned by a relatively peaceful period in the 440s, which saw treaties between Athens and Sparta signed for five years' peace in 445 BC and then for thirty years in 440 BC. The historical record of this period is almost completely reliant on Thucydides, who structures his narrative on a framework of 'great events' essentially consisting of warfare at some level and its attendant causes and outcomes. This history then presents a kaleidoscopic picture of alliances made and broken, expeditions predatory and punitive, victories and defeats, revolts and submissions. What it fails to depict, other than in an occasional aside is the continual growth in wealth and power that the empire achieved during this period. Some idea of the extent of this can be obtained by the record of phoros payments that was maintained in a very public and permanent manner by being chiselled into a *stele*, or stone pillar, which had four faces, set up in the Athenian *agora*, some fragments of which have survived. These show that typical figures for the number of cities paying the phoros each year were between one hundred and forty and one hundred and sixty-five. The figure varies each year, and the amount also varies for individual cities, indicating that payments were not always provided on time and were the subject of disputes and adjustments. (The payments were supposed to be brought to Athens during the annual festival of the Dyonisea and were incorporated into the dramatic programme of the festival by having the representatives of the paying cities literally depositing the coinage on stage with an audience present.) As the numbers of phoros payers suggest, the regular income to the Athenian state was considerable.

Despite this generally successful picture, there were some reversals. In 447 BC, The Athenians rather unusually re-entered Boeotia to put down oligarchic revolts against the Athenian alliance in a number of cities. The oligarchic forces, however, proved to be more resilient than anticipated, and themselves re-took Chaeronea, attacking the Athenian garrison, killing many and taking the rest as prisoners. The Athenians then appear to have decided that the well-established antipathy that the Boeotians had possessed for the Athenians for many years, certainly from before the Persian invasion, was simply too troublesome and agreed to evacuate Boeotia in return for the freeing of their imprisoned soldiers.

In 445 BC, the Euboeans revolted, and Pericles, as senior general, was dispatched there with an army. He had hardly arrived on the island before the news came that, in a somewhat suspicious piece of timing, the Megarians also had revolted, inviting Corinthian and other Peloponnesian troops to assist them in attacking the Athenian garrison there, which was 'slaughtered,' with only a few survivors. Pericles then withdrew his army from Euboea but was prevented from joining a small force that had been sent from Athens to Megara by a Spartan army that had marched into Attica, possibly to support the two revolts, and which had reached Eleusis, very close to Athens. The Athenian force sent to Megara contrived to bypass the Spartans, being helped by a local guide and reached Athens. When Pleistoanax, the Spartan king commanding the expedition, heard that Pericles' army had been thus reinforced and was on station in Athens, he realised that an attack on the city was unlikely to succeed and withdrew, returning to Sparta. (Once there, he was accused of accepting bribes to withdraw and was banished.) Pericles then returned to Euboea and reduced the island to submission, particularly concentrating the city of Histiaea in the north, which had been the scene of the massacre of the crew of an Athenian trireme some years before. The population was driven out, and the territory was handed over to Athenian colonists.

Following the reversals in Boeotia and Megara, the Athenians decided that it was better to concentrate on their mastery of the Aegean rather than attempting to establish a hegemonic position on the mainland and agreed to a thirty-year's peace with Sparta. This involved giving up their various possessions on the Saronic and Corinthian gulfs. This was a considerable humiliation for Athens, but for once, the attractions of peace appear to have overcome the expansionist ambitions of the state. One result of this was that Pericles was enabled to order a particularly lavish celebration of the Panathenaea festival in 442 BC.

This newly relaxed atmosphere was not to prevail for long, however, for in 440 BC, an oligarchic uprising overthrew the government of the island of Samos, Athens most powerful and faithful ally, and proclaimed a revolt from the Athenian Empire. The fact that the oligarchs had invited a Persian force commanded by the son of the governor of Sardis, a Persian stronghold, to assist them in their coup made the insurrection all the more threatening to the Athenians, who despatched a fleet of sixty ships under the command of Pericles to the island. Despite having to divert a number of his ships to the Asian coast to deal with a threat from the Phoenician fleet, which was under Persian control, the Athenians overcame a Samian fleet of seventy vessels, after which they landed an infantry force which defeated the oligarchic allies. Again, the threat of an attack by the Phoenician fleet was raised, and Pericles took the majority of the ships of the Athenians and their allies to confront it, leaving only a skeleton force. The Samians then regrouped and attacked this small Athenian force, overcoming them and becoming 'masters of their own coasts' for fourteen days. After this, Pericles returned and imposed a blockade, with reinforcements sent from Athens. The Samians attempted to fight off the Athenian force but failed and eventually submitted to the blockade. The terms of their capitulation were severe: they were to demolish their walls, give hostages, surrender their ships and pay a large indemnity by regular payments. In effect, they were reduced to the subject status from being an ally, contributing their considerable sea power to the confederation instead of paying the phoros. The severity of these exactions is perhaps surprising, given that the revolt was apparently inflicted on the general Samian population by a faction backed up by foreign troops and also the previous long-standing fidelity of the island state to Athens. It was typical, however, of the way in which the Athenians dealt with any hint of secession on the part of their 'allies.' Perhaps even more surprising is the fact that, despite this, the Samians remained loyal to Athens for most of the remainder of the century, including a period when many of their fellow subjects of the Empire took the opportunity presented by Athens' weakness to break free, and also played a significant part in the restoration of democratic rule in Athens after the revolt of 411 BC.

As the foregoing passages have attempted to portray, the Empire created by the transformation of the Athenians' leadership of the Delian League, assumed at the invitation of their allies, most of whom became their subjects, can only be described as a tyrannical hegemony. One which inevitably generated ill-feeling and the desire for freedom from the imperial yoke, at least in the upper echelons of many of the subject societies. To some extent, this dissatisfaction did not arise in the proletarian sections of these societies, who seemed to have maintained a fellow feeling for a regime in which, whatever its imperialist external policies, was directed by the expressed will of the

Athenian plethos. There was no doubt, however, that hatred of Athens was widespread in the politically active citizens of many Greek states, including many who were not subjected to Athenian rule. This hatred then provided fertile ground for the Spartans to develop their plans to destroy Athenian supremacy, gathering allies by their not entirely spurious claim to wish to free the Greeks from Athenian domination.

Chapter 4
The Creation of a Radical Democracy

The reforms of Kleisthenes, as described in Chapter 1, produced a democracy tolerated by the oligarchic factions of the upper classes but regarded as unsatisfactory by many, including democrats who were to be found also in these upper classes and who could influence the assembly.

In the four-sixties BC, the oligarchs' leader was Kimon, the commander-in-chief of the Delian League. Kimon, in common with many upper-class Athenians, was an admirer of Sparta and adopted a bi-lateral approach to political leadership in Greece, by which Sparta was recognised as the hegemon over the mainland, deriving from her military superiority on land, while Athens' superiority in naval warfare correspondingly made her 'mistress of the seas,' and, particularly, hegemony over the states in and around the Aegean – the 'two yoke-fellows' policy.

Consistent with his admiration of Sparta, a notably anti-democratic state, Kimon had little sympathy with any further advances in the democracy in Athens and was thus in opposition to Aristides, who favoured them and who was the most powerful voice in the assembly. On Aristides' death, Kimon was left as the most powerful statesman but was faced by a growing faction of democrats demanding further reforms. The leaders of this faction were Ephialtes and his lieutenant Pericles.

The single most significant obstacle in the way of further democratic reform was the Council of the Areopagos, which was established by Solon and constituted of ex-Archons, who were members for life once appointed. Archons, the senior public officials, were chosen from the two upper classes by lot but from a select group chosen by election, a process also used for other senior magistrates. In this, they were distinguished from other officers of state who were chosen by lot from the whole male citizen population. The Council was intended by Solon to act as custodian of the Athenian constitution, but by the 460s, had extended its powers by a wide interpretation of its remit to include involvement in the examination of public officials both before and after their year of office, and also general supervision of the city's affairs with the power to punish without giving reasons. Isocrates, the fourth-century BC rhetorician, describes the rule of the Council in almost Orwellian terms: 'Our ancestors kept watch over the lives of every citizen, dragging the disorderly before the Areopagos, which criticised, threatened or punished them as they deserved.' The Council was thus a self-perpetuating reactionary force, which operated entirely without accountability, as such cutting directly across a major principle of the democratic reforms of Ephialtes, that every public official and every state institution should be held accountable in public hearings by the *Heliaea,* or peoples' law courts, the Boule of 500 or, rarely, the Ekklesia.

The democrats, then, concentrated their energies on the emasculation of the Council of the Areopagos, aided initially by the absence of its chief supporter, Kimon, in his disastrous expedition to aid the Spartans in the Helot revolt, then followed by his unpopularity on his return as having put Athens in the position of being 'smote in the face' by the Spartans. The Council had been softened up by the traditional Athenian method of attacking and removing individual members of it in the law courts in a campaign conducted by Ephialtes. This engendered a general distrust of the Council in the populace at large, which, taken with Kimon's unpopularity, prepared the ground for stripping the Council of its powers, leaving it restricted to jurisdiction over religious crimes, notably murder (which was regarded as a religious offence because the shedding of blood was held to contaminate the city). The supervision of the constitution was transferred to the Boule of 500 and the Heliaea. The actions of the Council were subject to examination by the Boule. The significance of this downgrading of the Council was not lost on subsequent commentators, who were generally unsympathetic to what was seen as a dangerous experiment. Plutarch, for example, remarks that 'Ephialtes... who broke the power of the Areopagos, giving the people, according to Plato's expression, so copious and strong a draught of liberty that it grew wild and unruly like an unmanageable horse.'

Kimon attempted to lead a rear-guard action to reinstate the powers of the Areopagos, but he misjudged the mood of the people who, under the influence of their 'strong draught,' responded eagerly to the democrats' call for his ostracism and the necessary 6,000 votes were cast. Shortly after Kimon's ostracism, Ephialtes was assassinated, leaving Pericles as the leader of the democratic movement and 'first amongst equals' in the democracy.

The emasculation of the Areopagos left democracy under the control of three essentially democratic institutions: the Boule of 500, the Heliaea – the peoples' courts, and the Ekklesia – the assembly of the entire male citizen population. Ephialtes' reforms had placed the greater part of the responsibility for holding officials and institutions to account on the Heliaea, where cases often required a jury of 501, and thus necessitated a large number of jury members to be available. Any citizen could put himself forward as a prospective jury member, but this required frequent attendance, which was difficult or impossible for the lower classes – the zeugitai and thetes – who needed to work for a living. The notion of accountability being in the hands of the people was thus threatened by becoming biased towards the leisured classes. Recognising this, Pericles instituted payment for jury members, initially at the rate of two obols per day (an obol being worth one-sixth of a drachma – the standard daily rate for a workman). Although not permitting luxury, this was adequate to support an individual with a small family but was more intended as enough to compensate for the occasional loss of a few days' work.

Payment was also introduced for state officials, thus enabling the poorest in society to fulfil offices to which they were allocated by lot. This included payment for the position of Archon, which removed the financial barrier to members of the lower classes from assuming this role, and the office was opened to the zeugitai in 457 BC. There is no record of the thetes being formally permitted to the Archonship, but towards the second half of the fifth century, the distinction between the two lower classes was becoming blurred, and indeed, the Solonic classes seemed to have become obsolete, with some evidence of a general tendency to encourage the promotion of thetes to zeugitai, or 'the hoplite class.' Aristotle remarks that when candidates for public office were examined, they were asked from which Solonic class they came, and none replied 'thetikon' – from the thetes.

The 500 members of the Boule, which occupied a central role in the democratic administration, were not paid for their services initially, but by the time of the oligarchic revolt of 411 BC, when the Boule of 500 was abolished, its members were paid off up to the end of their period of service in a gesture intended to humiliate both them and the whole structure of paid officials and jurors. There is considerable discussion about exactly when the Boule members began to be paid.

The connexion between the navy and the radical democracy ushered in by Ephialtes' and Pericles' reforms was perceived by oligarchs and philosophers alike.

Aristotle remarks: 'For he [Pericles] took away some of the functions of the Areopagos, and he urged the state very strongly in the direction of naval power, *which resulted in emboldening the multitude*, who brought all the government more into their own hands'(Athenian Constitution XXVII).

An obvious implication of the democratic reforms is that they depended on a greatly increased level of expenditure borne by the state – a state, moreover, where there was no form of income tax. The level of state expenditure was already considerable as the result of the upkeep of the navy, which involved the construction and maintenance of the ships, to a certain extent offset by the contribution of the trierarchy and payment of the crews. There was some tax revenue from harbour and import taxes, but the greater part of the state's income was the phoros – the tribute paid annually by the members of the Delian League. The money accumulated by the phoros payments was originally intended to be devoted to the upkeep of the navy so that it could maintain the defence of the members of the Delian League against the Persian threat. However, the battle of Eurymedon had effectively removed this threat, and the Athenians, led by Pericles, felt justified in utilising what had become a large sum for wider purposes, mainly in support of democracy. This process was reinforced both practically and symbolically by removing the fund from the island of Delos to the Athenian Acropolis, where it was readily available. There were protests against this move, notably by Thucydides of Alopece, not the historian but a close relative of Kimon who had assumed the latter's role as spokesman of the anti-democrats on his death and who consistently opposed Pericles until he was ostracised. Pericles brushed aside these criticisms, saying that provided that the Athenians made good their commitment to defending them, the members of the Delian League had no right to dictate to what purpose their payments were put. In effect, this was a tacit statement of the transformation of the league into an empire, with the phoros being recognised as a tribute to Athens as hegemon rather than first among equals in a defence pact. The three entities – the democracy, the empire and the navy, were thus developing into an interlocking dependency: the democracy required largescale financial support, the empire was vital for the payment of the phoros, and the navy was essential to protect the empire from both external and internal threats, while the navy was itself dependent on financial support, and thus the support of the assembly, to agree its funding.

The relatively peaceful period from 450 BC to the onset of the Peloponnesian war in 431 BC allowed the 'Delian' fund to grow to a very considerable size. The existence of this large sum of money and its availability to the Athenians had profound consequences for the support both of the radical democracy, as noted above, but also of the culture that came to define the classical era. Thus, Plutarch comments (*Life of Pericles*, IX): 'that the people were first led on by him [Pericles] into allotments of public lands, festival-grants, and distributions of fees for public services.' The allotments and fees were part of the democratisation programme, while festivals, which provided the breeding ground of poetry and drama and had been supported by rich *liturgoi*, became the property of the *demos*. In addition, the money was used for the construction of the architectural wonders that were to make Athens famous for many centuries, as Plutarch indicates (XII): "That which alone now testifies for Hellas that her ancient power and splendour, of which so much is told, was no idle fiction—I mean his construction of sacred edifices, this, more than all the public measures of Pericles, his enemies maligned and slandered.

They cried out in the assemblies: "The people have lost their fair fame and are in ill repute because it has removed the public money of the Hellenes from Delos into its own keeping."

Pericles' consistent critic, Thucydides, added his condemnation: "Greece cannot but resent it as an insufferable affront, and consider herself to be tyrannized over openly when she sees the treasure, which was contributed by her upon a necessity for the war, wantonly lavished out by us upon our city, to guild her all over, and to adorn and set her forth, as it were some vain woman, hung around with precious stones and figures and temples, which cost a world of money."

It seems probable that these criticisms were unlikely to resonate with many Athenians, the majority of whom would at least have welcomed the replacement of the temples that were destroyed during the Persian occupation, particularly that of Athene, the titular god of the city. The Athenians (with a very few exceptions), in common with most of the Greeks, took their relationship with their gods very seriously, and the destruction of Athene's temple was held to dishonour her and the city, and so its replacement was both a matter of civic pride and a guarantee of good fortune. The new temple, which became known as the Parthenon, was perhaps the most iconic of all the edifices resulting from this great construction programme, with its noble proportions and design, its commanding position on the Acropolis, and the huge statue of the goddess that resided in it. This statue, created by the sculptor Phidias, was a wooden structure clad in gold and ivory – the ivory representing the immortal flesh and the gold covering of the figure.

What is perhaps surprising is that an important secondary motivation that resulted in the creation of these magnificent structures was essentially social. There had been a considerable increase in the population of the city as the result of the migration of particularly agricultural workers from the rural areas encouraged by, amongst others, Aristides. This, in turn, had led to the growth of un or under-employed poor, who tended to fall into crime or other anti-social behaviour. In response to this problem, "He boldly suggested to the people projects for great constructions, and designs for works which would call many arts into play and involve long periods of time, in order that the stay-at-homes, no whit less than the sailors and sentinels and soldiers, might have a pretext for getting a beneficial share of the public wealth" (Plutarch, *Life of Pericles*, XIII).

To summarise: the democracy that was developed over a century and a half and brought to its advanced, or radical, state that emancipated the *Plethos*, the common people of the city, by Ephialtes and Pericles, and which has given the world not only a perhaps inimitable model of democracy but also a rich legacy of drama and philosophy together with at least the images of architectural grandeur, was supported by an empire maintained and controlled by force manifested in its navy which was itself largely manned by the *Plethos*.

Chapter 5
The Prelude to the Archidamian War

Towards the end of the four hundred and thirties BC, it became ever more obvious that Sparta's offended *amour propre* and fear resulting from the apparently unstoppable increase in power and influence of the Athenian Empire were going to lead to war. In fact, Athens had experienced a number of setbacks in the preceding decade, notably including the failure to hold onto her attempted incursions into the mainland in Boeotia and the northern fringes of the Peloponnese. These, however, had not mollified the Spartans, despite the thirty-years peace agreed between the two powers in four hundred and forty-five BC. Indeed the period of comparative peace that had followed its signing had seemed to have acted as a pressure cooker, boiling up the Spartans' resentment against a state whose naval power had enabled it to, as they liked to characterise it, enslave many Greek cities, claiming a hegemonic position and casting Sparta's own self-image as the leading power of the Hellenes into the shade. The result was an overwhelming urge to divest the Athenians of their Empire, thus to reduce them to the level of an 'ordinary' state, by threats and diplomacy if possible, but by warfare if necessary. In this ambition, the Spartans were by no means alone. They were the recognised leader of the Peloponnesians, notably including the Corinthians, who all, with a few exceptions, followed the Spartan line, but many other Greek states, including those who had never been subjected to Athenian rule, supported them, reflecting the 'Universal hatred and fear of the Athenians.' Indeed, according to Thucydides (II, 8), 'All Hellas was excited by the coming conflict between her two chief cities.' The respective youth of Peloponnesus and Athens, who had grown up in an unusually peaceful period, 'had never seen war' and were infected by war fever and eager to take up arms.

Despite this widespread conviction that war was inevitable, its actual onset had to be delayed until there was a blatant breach of the peace treaty still in force. Treaties, which were backed by oaths sworn to the gods, were not lightly set aside, and the two potentially warring parties were keen to avoid the accusation of disrespect to the gods implicit in an abrogation, resembling two wild-west gunfighters, each willing the other to draw first. A potential trigger event occurred in 432 BC when a dispute between Corinth and one of its colonies, Corcyra (modern Corfu), reached the stage of threatening military action, for which both, having sizeable navies, were well prepared. The Corcyreans, in a bid for Athenian help, asked to join as an ally, saying that with their naval resources, they would contribute to an even more powerful force. Not unnaturally, the Corinthians wished to prevent this, reminding the Athenians that they had made twenty triremes available to them before Salamis and also that when the Peloponnesians had been minded to come to the assistance of Samos when it had revolted against Athens, they had voted not to do so, maintaining that 'everyone should be able to chastise their own allies,' claiming a clear parallel with their dispute with Corcyra.

The Athenians devoted two assemblies to discuss the Corcyreans' request and decided to accede to it, motivated by the desire to avoid the Corcyrean navy falling into the Corinthians' hands. However, in an attempt to avoid an accusation of breaking the treaty, which could certainly be justifiably made if Athenian and Corinthian ships actually fought, the agreement with Corcyra was for mutual defence only so that the Athenians would act only if Corcyrean ships were attacked, for which purpose they sent ten ships to Corcyra. Despite this, the Corinthians went ahead and attacked the Corcyreans when the Athenians were with them, but they took part only when a Corcyrean ship was hard-pressed and then apparently only threatening rather than actually engaging. After some initial success, the Corcyreans were falling back when the Corinthians broke away, having seen twenty Athenian ships that had been sent as reinforcements arriving, apparently to join the engagement. On the next day, the Corcyreans and Athenians sailed to where the Corinthians were anchored in anticipation of a continuation of the action. The Corinthians weighed anchor and came out but did not attempt to join battle, instead sending a small boat under a flag of truce to ask the Athenians what their intentions were. They maintained that they were there only to defend Corcyra and that if the Corinthians wished to sail anywhere else, they would not interfere with them. The Corinthians duly departed but then accused the Athenians of breaking the treaty by fighting with the Corcyreans against them, but this seems not to have convinced the Peloponnesians generally.

The next potential flashpoint occurred when the Corinthians managed to persuade another of their colonies, Potidaea, which had become a 'Tributary and ally of Athens,' to revolt against their Athenian allegiance. The Athenians sent a force to quell the revolt, which, after considerable efforts, invaded Potidaea and applied the usual strict measures to its inhabitants. Both sides then claimed that the other had broken the treaty: the Peloponnesians on the grounds that Athens had invaded a Corinthian colony, the Athenians that the Corinthians had stirred up the revolt in their ally.

Following this perceived provocation, the Spartans called a conference of their Peloponnesian allies, seizing the opportunity to canvas a war against Athens. Under the Spartan chairmanship, the Corinthians were particularly vociferous in support of war, but also others, notably the Aeginetans and Megarians, responded to the Spartans' invitation for any state with a grievance against Athens to come forward. The Aeginetans complained that they had been robbed of their independence, and the Megarians that they faced starvation, having been excluded from all harbours under the Athenian dominion and the Athens market as the result of the 'Megarian decree' passed by the Athenian assembly as a punishment for perceived Megarian duplicity.

In the subsequent debate, the Corinthians took the lead. Thucydides provides a reconstruction of their representative's speech (I, 70), which began with a description of the unique qualities of their common enemy, contrasting the dash and impetuosity of the Athenians, their restless desire to succeed and dominate with the dilatoriness, reluctance to act even when in imminent danger, and lack of initiative of the Spartans – the hegemon of the Peloponnesians. He went on to accuse the Spartans of failing to end the 'slavery' of Athens' victims by their lack of action. The Peloponnesians, if they acted in unity, would be more than a match for Athens. He then broached the inevitable issue of Athens' naval strength, claiming that this was based only on mercenaries who could easily be bought off, the money for which 'must be found,' even if this meant 'borrowing' from the treasury at the shrine at Delphi. At the same time, the Peloponnesians must build their own navy to challenge Athenian maritime dominance. With perhaps more realism, he suggested that Athens' allies could easily be persuaded to revolt against their tyrannical overlord, finally suggesting that a failure to act against, as he put it, the enslavement of Greece would render the Peloponnesians deserving of enslavement themselves.

An Athenian embassy, which by chance happened to be there on other business, was allowed to speak in answer. They reminded the assembly of Marathon and Salamis, benefitting all the Hellenes, then asked why their having an empire made them 'deserve to be so bitterly hated?' They reminded the conference that they had assumed leadership of the allies against Persia only when invited to do so after the Spartans had pulled out. They pointed out that the Spartans 'manage the cities of Peloponnesus to suit your own views' (by installing oligarchies Thucydides I, 76). They also suggested that the Spartans, because of their unique institutions, were unsuited to empire, and in any case, if they supplanted the Athenian empire with their own, they, in turn, would be hated. They urged that their differences should be submitted to arbitration according to the Treaty; if the Spartans refused, then the Athenians claimed they would be the authors of the war, as witnessed by the gods, 'by whom your oaths were sworn.'

These arguments, however, produced no sympathetic response in the Peloponnesian assembly, which went on to vote in favour of war with Athens.

The Spartans were still reluctant to be the first to strike and attempted to provoke the Athenians into action by sending a number of embassies, making demands that they knew would be unacceptable. Initially, they demanded that the Athenians 'drive out the curse of the Goddess,' which was a coded way of saying 'Banish Pericles.' The underlying story involved an incident in the sixth century BC when an Olympic hero named Cylon attempted to seize power as a tyrant of Athens. The coup was rapidly put down, and Cylon fled to distant parts. Some of his followers, however, failed to follow his example and were trapped on the Acropolis, where they sought sanctuary in the temple of Athene. They were persuaded to give themselves up by a promise that no harm would come to them. Despite this, they were summarily executed, a disgraceful event with the extremely serious result of defiling the temple of Athene – the tutelary deity of Athens. Responsibility for the crime was imputed to the Alcmaeonids, a powerful aristocratic family who were banished in consequence. The family was rehabilitated fairly rapidly and returned with its head, Kleisthenes, then being the originator of the revised tribal system in Athens that underpinned the development of democracy in the state. The connection with Pericles was via his mother, who was of the clan. As Thucydides says (II 126), the Spartans did not really expect that the Athenians would exile Pericles but hoped to discredit him, a somewhat forlorn hope given Pericles' popularity at this time. In response, the Athenians demanded that the Spartans take appropriate action to placate Athene after her temple in Sparta had been defiled by the starving to death there of Pausanias, the renegade victor of Plataea.

After a year or so of this phoney near-war, the inevitable trigger event happened at the somewhat unlikely location of Plataea, a city in Boeotia but maintaining an allegiance with Athens rather than Thebes, the capital city of Boeotia. The two cities, despite their geographical closeness, being only some eight miles apart, had been divided by a historic quarrel, and the Thebans decided to have a final reckoning with the Plataeans, encouraged by a pro-Theban faction who undertook to open the gates of the city to a Theban invasion. The Thebans entered the city during darkness, and the inhabitants, being completely surprised, offered no resistance. The Thebans, rather than taking advantage of this by taking control, remained in the *agora* where they had gathered and urged the Plataeans to throw their lot in with Thebes, their natural ally. Having got over their original stupefaction, the Plataeans rapidly discovered that the Theban force was quite limited in size and, still under cover of darkness, began to organise resistance. On the first light of dawn, the Thebans were attacked not only by armed bands but also by the general populace, including the women, who rained down tiles and imprecations from the rooftops on the invaders as they attempted to escape from the city. Eventually, those Thebans who survived were taken prisoner, and a backup force that had been sent from Thebes in the expectation of an unopposed occupation experienced difficulties occasioned by the river Asopus, which had been swollen by the heavy rain that had fallen throughout the episode and arrived late only to discover the Plataeans on full alert and clearly in no mood for submission. The Plataeans forestalled any further Theban action by sending out a herald to protest at their unjustified attack in a time of peace and to warn them against touching anything or body outside the city walls, threatening to execute the prisoners if they did so. According to the Thebans, they swore an oath to leave the prisoners unharmed if the force withdrew, though this was denied by the Plataeans. When the Athenians heard of the Theban action, they sent a force to support the Plataeans, having first sent a messenger to tell them not to kill the prisoners. This, however, came too late as the Plataeans had executed them as soon as the Thebans had retreated. Whatever the rights and wrongs of the affair, it was clear that the peace had been broken and that war was now inevitable. The Spartans sent a final embassy with the message that 'The Lacedaemonians [Spartans] desire to maintain peace; and peace there may be if you will restore independence to the Hellenes,' in other words, 'Give up your Empire.'

The Athenian assembly met to consider the Peloponnesians' message with the intention of arriving at a final decision to end this sequence of threatening uncertainty. Many views were expressed both for and against hostilities. Eventually, Pericles spoke. He began by counselling against acceding to some of the more immediate Peloponnesian demands, instancing the revocation of the Megarian decree, which excluded the Megarians effectively from commercial activities within the Athenian Empire. This had been mentioned in the preceding debate as a fairly trivial matter that might be acquiesced to if it resulted in the maintenance of peace. Pericles insisted that this would simply be interpreted as a sign of weakness, and lead to ever more demands until a red line was reached that the Athenians could never accept, leading to the outbreak of war, which was what the Peloponnesians were bent on, as demonstrated by their refusal to go to arbitration. He then went on to consider the ability of Peloponnesians, particularly the Spartans, to sustain a lengthy war, which was ultimately dependent on money – warfare being, above all, a great consumer of wealth. He characterised them as essentially subsisting on the land with no treasuries held by their administrations, in comparison with which Athens possessed very large monetary resources and was still receiving the annual tribute from her extensive empire. It was also the case that the Peloponnesians had little experience of warfare away from their immediate localities, whereas the Athenians, with their imperial experience, were pre-eminent in projecting power anywhere where their navy could reach. He also ridiculed the idea that the Peloponnesians might rapidly develop a capacity for naval warfare that would challenge Athens' command of the seas, pointing out that the Athenians' mastery had been built on the experience of over half a century since the victory at Salamis, and that they were not dependent on mercenaries to crew their ships, even if the Peloponnesians carried out their plan to take money from the treasury of the shrine at Delphi to tempt the mercenaries away with promises of higher pay, which would fail in any case. He emphasised the importance of the navy, in that the Athenians must avoid meeting the Peloponnesians in a pitched land battle, where they would be outnumbered, but use their naval power to inflict damage and losses on their coastal areas while protecting Athens as an island fortified by the walls that isolated it from the land. He proclaimed his conviction that Athens' intrinsic strength and wealth would bring them to victory, warning only that he feared that their own mistakes rather than the enemy's efforts might result in defeat, and cautioned particularly against attempting to extend the empire while engaged in a war that threatened their survival. Finally, he recommended that the assembly tell the Peloponnesian embassy to take back the reply that the Athenians would revoke the Megarian decree if Sparta would permit foreigners to live and trade in their territory (the Spartans would frequently eject foreigners for no apparent reason other than their foreignness), that they would restore independence to cities if it could be shown that they had been independent prior to the signing of the Treaty, that they would 'free' the Hellenes from their empire if the Spartans would cease to impose oligarchies on their allies, and they once again requested that their differences should be considered by arbitration as specified by the Treaty. The assembly voted to follow Pericles' advice, the ambassadors left with this message and never returned.

With war still undeclared, both sides began to look to their allies for commitment to support in the forthcoming hostilities. The Spartans had the benefit of the almost complete support of the Peloponnesian states, together with their traditional allies close to Attica, including the Boeotians and Megarans. By contrast, Athens' allies, with the exception of Plataea, were scattered around Greece and the Aegean, such as Corcyra, and the island states of Chios and Samos. Having gathered his allies together, Archidamos, the Spartan king whose name has been associated with this first part of the Peloponnesian war, determined to invade Attica in the hope that the Athenians, recognising the threat of their lands and townships outside the city itself being 'laid to waste' by a powerful invasion force would see sense and sue for peace. He assured his assembled commanders that if the Athenians did not, they would be unable to watch their country's properties and communities being destroyed without coming out from their fortifications and confronting them, at which their military supremacy would give the Peloponnesians victory.

Pericles' response to the invasion was to insist that the inhabitants of the 'Greater Athens' in rural Attica must evacuate their homesteads and townships and relocate to the city of Athens, where they would be protected by the walls, which were guarded continuously, and the navy on the seafront. With considerable reluctance, a large proportion of the threatened population did move into the city, bringing whatever they could carry with them. Those with cattle had them taken to Euboea. Very few of them were able to lodge with relatives or friends. The remainder found shelter in temples and shrines or huts or even in the open with some protection afforded by the long walls. Pericles insisted that when the invaders finally reached the city walls, there must be no attempt to form a line of battle against them, despite the likelihood that those from the nearest farms and villages would have to watch as their properties were ravaged.

In a last attempt to obtain peace that would satisfy the Peloponnesians, Archidamos sent a single individual to Athens in the hope that the realisation that his army was on its way would persuade the inhabitants. But the assembly had already agreed on a motion proposed by Pericles to the effect that they would receive no embassy or herald as long as Archidamos' army was operational, and Melesippos, the man sent, was refused entry to the city and escorted to the state boundary.

Thus began the Peloponnesian war, or more specifically, its first phase, the Archidamian war. The entire conflict was to last twenty-eight years, with one brief truce. During the war, the Athenian democracy was severely threatened twice and was eventually left weakened to a shadow of its former greatness.

Chapter 6
The Archidamian War

This chapter is not intended to give an exhaustive description of the war but rather to attempt to cover the major incidents and individuals that were most significant in its progress.

With the last attempt to persuade the Athenians to sue for peace having failed, despite the threat of imminent hostilities, the Peloponnesian army continued its invasion of Attica in a fairly leisurely manner, attracting a certain amount of criticism to Archidamos from some of his allies who argued that this had given the Athenians the time to vacate their hinterland when they could have been caught unprepared. They reached and ravaged Eleusis, close enough to Athens to be reached by an annual procession, where the Athenians hoped they would halt their progress as a previous Peloponnesian incursion fourteen years before under Pleistoanax, another Spartan king, had done. However, Archidamos moved inexorably on into Acharnae, an outer suburb of the city, where they encamped and continued their laying waste to whatever they found, in the expectation that the Athenians would come out and meet them. In this, they were disappointed – there was no sign of any opposition, apart from occasional sallies by the Athenian cavalry intercepting scouting parties if they came close to the city walls. The inhabitants of Acharnae, who were quite numerous, having supplied some three thousand hoplites for the defence of the city, in which they were now sequestered, were only too aware of the destruction that was being visited on their homes and farms and rapidly became understandably angry at Pericles' policy of non-confrontation and urged a full-blooded armed response. Pericles refused any change to his policy, and the Acharnians, with a sullen reluctance, had to comply.

Something of the anger of the Acharnians is featured in Aristophanes' comedy *'The Acharnians,'* which won first prize at the Linaean festival in 426 BC. The comedy centres around an Athenian named Dicaeopolis who, tired of the war, decide to agree a personal treaty with the Spartans, sending a friend, Amphitheus, with eight drachmas to negotiate it. In a remarkably short time, the friend returns with three alternative treaties, but he is being pursued by a crowd of elderly Acharnians, who form the chorus. They are incensed at the idea of a treaty with the Spartans and who proclaim: 'Old Acharnians like ourselves shall not be set at nought by a scoundrel who has dared, great Gods! to conclude a truce when I wanted the war continued with double fury in order to avenge my ruined lands. No mercy for our foes until I have pierced their hearts like a sharp reed so that they dare never again ravage my vineyards.' Aristophanes' comedy reflects the war-weariness of the Athenians after six years, being fortunately unconscious of the twenty or so more years that it was to endure.

The Peloponnesians, having failed to provoke a confrontation with the Athenians, left Acharnae and moved into the area north of the city, ravaging as they went and then, having exhausted their provisions, returned to their cities travelling back through Boeotia. As this invasion was proceeding, the Athenians sent one hundred triremes, one-third of their naval strength, to raid the Peloponnesian coast.

This expedition perhaps represented a new form of warfare for the Athenians in being essentially an amphibious force intended for land attack rather than a straightforward naval operation. The ships carried one thousand hoplites (heavy-armed) and four hundred archers, who were landed at target locations to conduct short but destructive forays before re-embarking and continuing the ravaging elsewhere. During one of these episodes, where they attacked a fortress at Methone, they were confronted by a small force of Spartans led by one Brasidas, who ignored the activity around the fortress and went to secure the city of Methone. Brasidas was to become a thorn in the Athenians' side (and Thucydides' in particular) later in the decade. After they had returned, the fleet was again in action in a more conventional invasion of Aegina, the island close to the Peloponnesian coast, lying over from Athens in the Saronic Gulf. The action was thoroughgoing, motivated by the Athenians' belief that the Aeginetans had been instrumental in fomenting the war and resulted in the expulsion of the entire population, which was replaced by Athenian settlers. The exiled Aeginetans were given a town to occupy by the Spartans.

These water-borne operations did not comprise the full extent of Athens' response to the Peloponnesian invasion: a large land force invaded Megara, the nearest Peloponnesian ally, under the leadership of Pericles. After 'ravaging the greater part of the country,' they retired, establishing a pattern that was repeated in subsequent years.

In passing, it might seem surprising that Pericles, apparently a senior political figure and statesman in Athens, should lead a military expedition with all the risks that this entailed. The point to grasp is that the Athenian assembly had no parties, party leaders, or indeed 'government.' Pericles, like any other citizen, spoke in response to a general summons from an officiating herald: 'Who wishes to speak?' His presence in the assembly and the respect given to his views by it was the result of his long and successful membership of the board of generals, the only public office that could be held for more than a single year, but most of all by his great talent for oratory. His enemies often claimed that his prominence was akin to a tyranny, but this accusation was difficult to sustain. As senior general, he would be the natural choice to lead such a largescale expedition.

Following the usual pattern in the ancient world, the war was suspended with the onset of winter. During the winter, the Athenians held their annual funeral ceremony for the war dead. It was customary for a prominent citizen to deliver an oration, and in this first winter of the war, the choice fell on Pericles to speak. This *epitaphios logos* has become a model for similar occasions ever since, including, for example, Lincoln's Gettysburg Address. In it, Pericles maintains that the Athenians' valour, which was universally recognised, arose from their pride in their democratic system and the openness of their society, which gave the city its greatness rather than from an obsession with war and conquest.

With the subsequent summer came the next Peloponnesian invasion of Attica, again led by Archidamos. This time, however, the danger of the invasion was dwarfed by a new enemy – an outbreak of plague. Despite many attempts, nobody has been able to provide an identification of this infestation that has been generally accepted. The one certainty is that it was not malaria; it was far too infectious (malaria requires the mediation of the *anopheles* mosquito to spread rather than simple human-to-human contact). In the over-crowding of the city and the area within the walls resulting from the evacuation of the Attic countryside, the plague found itself in ideal conditions for a wildfire spread through the population. With the first wave of fatalities went the physicians, whose inevitable proximity to the sick and dying made them highly vulnerable. In their absence, the people resorted to praying to the gods in the temples before these became choked with bodies, those of both the supplicants and the refugees who had sought shelter there. The course and effects of the disease are described in some detail by Thucydides, the historian who was one of the few who contracted it and survived. The initial effect was a sensation of hotness in the head, which then spread down the body with varied and distressing results at each stage, with death often following rapidly, probably coming as a relief to many. The numbers rapidly overcame any attempts to observe the normal funeral procedures, and the city and its environs were littered with pyres on which the bodies were burnt without ceremony or even identification.

In the midst of these two serious afflictions, the Peloponnesian invasion and the plague, the Athenians, in what may be regarded as either defiant resilience or foolhardiness, sent a large force, again of one hundred ships, but this time with four thousand hoplites and three hundred cavalry, for which old triremes were converted into horse transports, and again to ravage the Peloponnesian coast, under the command of Pericles. On its return, the fleet was redeployed with a new commander, Hagnon, and sailed to Potidaea to attempt to bring the siege there, which was still being maintained by a small army under Phormio, to a successful conclusion. Despite strenuous efforts and the use of siege engines, they did not prevail. This was largely because they had brought the plague with them, and the besieging force was rapidly weakened by the spread of the infection. When Hagnon returned to Athens, he had lost fifteen hundred of the four thousand hoplites originally embarked.

At this juncture, the spirit of the Athenians, understandably, suffered a downturn, having been exposed both to the plague and the widespread ravaging of the Attic countryside. Inevitably, they sought a scapegoat for their discontent, and also this was inevitably focused on Pericles – he had persuaded them to go to war and prevented them from defending their properties in the country, and his policy of bringing the rural population into the city had resulted in the over-crowding that allowed the plague to spread so destructively. He was also attacked for his friendship with the philosopher Anaxagoras, whose views on the reality and power of the gods were regarded as heretical by the Athenian populace, whose theological conservatism had been augmented by the plague – seen as a sign of the Olympians' displeasure. Anaxagoras was prosecuted for impiety and apparently condemned to death, although he was spirited away to Lampsacos by Pericles before the sentence was carried out.

Pericles responded to these attacks with a 'more in sorrow than anger' speech, in which he said that he had anticipated the people's anger against him but reminded them that they, in the assembly, had agreed with all his decisions. He maintained that the loss of the houses, farms and estates owned by the citizens was preferable to the loss of the city itself, which would have dire results for all the populace. The properties would be rebuilt, but defeat would result in the destruction of the entire city, never to be recreated. He urged them to refrain from making peace overtures to the Spartans, which had happened and which had been rejected, insisting that these would only be interpreted as weakness and encourage the enemy. In the end, the assembly was sufficiently mollified to prevent it from adopting any major resolutions countering Pericles' policies, although they fined him. Consistent with the mercurial tendencies of the radical democracy, they then elected him to the Board of Generals for a further year.

Pericles died shortly afterward, a victim, it was said, of the plague, although he did not die quickly, and it seems rather questionable as to whether this was the actual cause. He was a very great democratic leader and statesman and was and is often contrasted with the subsequent 'leaders' of democratic Athens, who tend to be disparagingly referred to as 'demagogues.' The term originally simply meant 'leader of the people,' without the pejorative loading now attached to it, which, however, appeared relatively early as the result of the perceived contrast of men such as Cleon, whose demeanour in the assembly was loud and aggressive by contrast with Pericles' dignified and moderate presence. It might be noted that Aristotle, no friend of democracy, referred to Pericles as a demagogue and also that Cleon's policies, despite his bombast, were very similar to those of Pericles.

Later in the summer, the focus of the hostilities switched to the western coast of Greece, where the Spartans began to attack Athenian allies, particularly those remote from Athens but comparatively close to their Peloponnesian allies. An amphibious force of one hundred ships and one thousand hoplites under the Spartan admiral Cnemos attacked the island of Zacynthos, which, although a Peloponnese colony, was an ally of Athens. Despite the invasion force landing and ravaging the greater part of the country, the Zacynthians refused to submit, and eventually, they sailed away.

At much the same time, an ominous development saw Spartan ambassadors together with Aristaeus, a Corinthian who had led the resistance to Athens in Potidaea, attempt to approach the king of Persia with a view to persuading him to provide them with money and military assistance in the war. Somewhat unwisely, they made their objective known when they visited the court of Sitalces of Thrace, who was friendly towards Athens and who, at the time, was being visited by Athenian envoys. On hearing of the Spartans' plan, the Athenians asked Sitalces to hand the ambassadors over to them, reminding him that his son had been given Athenian citizenship and that his visitors plainly meant to disadvantage Athens. Sitalces was persuaded and handed them over, whence they were put on a ship to Athens and executed as soon as they were landed. The Athenians' justification for this action was the somewhat questionable one that the Spartans had, it was claimed, been in the habit of executing the crews of merchant ships of states not specifically allied to the Peloponnesians. The action did remove the threat of Persian intervention for a while, although it was an unwelcome indication of Spartan intentions.

Later in the year, a straightforward sea battle took place, in which the Spartans had an opportunity to exercise their new-found interest in marine warfare. The battle took place near the port city of Naupactos, at the western end of the Corinthian Gulf, and thus on the far side of mainland Greece from Athens, indicating the long reach of the Athenian navy. Naupactos, rather surprisingly, was an Athenian ally as the result of its having been populated by helots freed from the Spartans with Athenian help after their revolt in 462 BC. The Corinthian Gulf, which nearly joins the Saronic Gulf near the city of Corinth, and thus almost isolates the Peleponnese as a true island, narrows into a short strait just west of Naupactos, which leads into the open sea. The Athenians had sent Phormio, last mentioned as leading the siege of Potidaea, which had finally been ended with the surrender of the city, with twenty ships to keep station off Naupactos to disrupt shipping going to and from Corinth. The troop-carrying Peloponnesian fleet under the command of the Spartan Cnemos, with some forty-seven ships, approached Naupactos and were attacked by Phormio despite the numerical disparity. The immediate response of the Peloponnesians was to adopt the standard defensive manoeuvre of forming a circle of the ships, with their prows pointing radially outwards, with smaller vessels inside the circle. The Athenians then circled around the formation increasingly closely, and the Peloponnesians backed until, inevitably, they began to foul each other, losing their shape, allowing the Athenians to pick off stragglers as they became detached. Eventually, the Peloponnesians fled through the strait to the west and anchored in Calydon, leaving some twelve ships captured by the Athenians and others wrecked.

The Peloponnesians were understandably demoralised by this mauling by a numerically inferior force, and commissioners, including the ever more visible Brasidas, were sent from Sparta to advise Cnemos before his next confrontation with the enemy. When this occurred, in an action that started in the straits west of Naupactos, the fortunes were reversed, at least at the beginning. The Peloponnesian fleet, now augmented to seventy ships, appeared to be making for Naupactos, which Phormio had left undefended, and so he was forced to direct his fleet back towards the port, his ships sailing in line astern. The enemy followed rapidly and began to overhaul and attack the Athenian ships, nine of which were driven ashore and some captured, while eventually eleven were clear and approaching the port and safety. The last one of these was also on the point of being caught, and so its commander, in a defiant gesture, wheeled round behind a passing merchant ship and rammed the leader of his pursuers, which was some way ahead of its fellows, and sank it. The effect of this on the Peloponnesians was dramatic – their triumphant spirits evaporated, and they ceased rowing, collapsing into a confused melee. The Athenians, about to go into harbour seeing this, reversed their course and attacked the dispirited opposition who fled to Corinth, confirming that despite their ability to assemble fleets of warships, the Spartans still lacked the self-confidence in marine warfare that animated the Athenians.

The next major chapter of the war was centred on the revolt of the cities of the island of Lesbos, with the exception of Methymniaea, against Athenian 'tyranny,' being led by the important city of Mytilene, which had a significant fleet and had been one of Athens' most powerful allies. The revolt of the Mytileneans seems to have been devised and supported by the oligarchic element of the population and was articulated by them as a response to what they claimed as the unjust conversion of the Delian League into an imperial hegemony by the

Athenians, as the result of which they were now dragged into a war with Sparta by an Athens weakened by the plague and hence placing additional demands upon them. They sent embassies to both Athens and Sparta to obtain acquiescence or support for their desire for independence. The Athenians refused to engage in any discussion of a possible release of Mytilene from their empire and sent one thousand hoplites, who 'manned their own ships' unusually, under the general Paches to subdue the insurrection. This force represented a riposte to the idea of Athens being enfeebled by the plague, as it coincided with another raiding party of one hundred ships that attacked the Peloponnesians in the isthmus; this meant that a total of two hundred and fifty Athenian ships were simultaneously in action. Even for Athens, this was a considerable drain on resources, and for the first time, a property tax was levied on the wealthier Athenians, raising two hundred Talents. The leading light in the debates on this was the demagogue Cleon, who was to become a significant and voluble voice throughout the period.

The embassy to Sparta, by contrast, had a potentially positive result. The Spartans promised to send forty ships to support the revolt, which would follow the immediate dispatch of a Spartan named Salaethos, who would organise the liaison with the Spartan force when it arrived. Salaethos was successfully smuggled into the island from a single ship that eluded the Athenian force, which was by then engaged in besieging the city and port of Mytilene. Time went by, and the Athenians relentlessly tightened their grip, with the inevitable starvation, particularly of the poorer sections of the population, while the promised Spartan fleet failed to appear. Eventually, the oligarchic leaders of the revolt attempted to distribute weapons to the common people so that they could join them in a desperate sally to raise the siege, having given up hope of Spartan assistance. The people, however, refused to go along with this, claiming that the oligarchs had not shared their food with them, and so they were unwilling to join them in what anyway would almost certainly be a forlorn hope. The oligarchs were left with no alternative but to seek terms with Paches. This they did, offering to capitulate if Paches would agree to take no action against them until the matter had been considered by the Athenian assembly. He agreed to the terms and also permitted the Mytileneans to send ambassadors to argue their case at the assembly. He also sent the ringleaders of the revolt to Athens, together with the hapless Salaetheus.

The subsequent meeting of the assembly revealed the anger of the Athenian populace at what they saw as the treachery of the Mytileneans, who had not only revolted against Athens but also actively solicited the assistance of her bitter enemy. Spurred on by Cleon, the assembly agreed on the most extreme of the range of punishments conventionally inflicted on defeated cities. All adult males would be put to the sword, and the women and children sold into slavery. The resulting decree was indited, and a copy put on board a trireme, which sailed immediately for Mytilene as instructions to Paches for action.

On the morning of the following day, when tempers had cooled somewhat, the popular sentiment began to question the severity of the decision, and this grew to such an extent that another assembly was demanded to reconsider and was held later in the day. As on the previous day, Cleon, with characteristic vehemence, demanded condign punishment, justifying it by echoing Pericles' admission that the Empire was a tyranny, of necessity requiring the ruthless application of power to hold its subjects under its rule. Any sign of weakness would result in an outbreak of revolts. Cleon was opposed by Diodotus, who suggested that Cleon's grasp of *realpolitik* was jejune. Threatening insurrections with cruelty only served to harden the resistance of rebels and, in the case of Mytilene, would only leave a wrecked city, unable to pay the tribute on which Athens was so dependent. He also pointed out that the popular party in Mytilene, as in every other of the cities in the empire, was not against Athens, as demonstrated by their refusal to join the oligarchs, which had precipitated the surrender. He recommended that the executions be restricted to those already held in Athens, and the rest of the population left alone. Diodotos won the day, and another trireme was dispatched with orders countermanding the previous decree. The crew of the ship was provided with special rations by the Mytilenean ambassadors, and they rowed through day and night to attempt to overtake the first. Although they failed to catch the first trireme at sea, the bearer of the later decree managed to reach Paches as he was about to put the first into action. Although avoiding the extremes of the initial decree, the full terms of the punishment were severe enough. The Mytileneans lost their fleet and were forced to demolish the defensive walls of the city, while the territory of Lesbos was divided up and distributed amongst the Athenian population either as absentee landlords or occupying cleruchs.

Turning again to Athenian activity to the west of the Greek mainland, in 425 BC, a combination of one man's obsession and the forces of nature led to what might have been a trivial incident developing into a long-running affair involving two significant deaths, terminated only by a brief cessation of the war. The initial trigger for this chain of events was the revolt of the Sicilian city of Messene against Athenian rule. The revolt was inspired and supported by the most powerful Sicilian city, Syracuse, whose citizens, in what was to be revealed as a significant portent a decade later, were increasingly disturbed by Athens' influence on the island. In response, the Athenian assembly sent forty triremes under the joint command of Demosthenes and Eurymedon to quell the revolt. In their voyage, these ships met severe weather conditions off the South Western point of the Peloponnese and were obliged to shelter in a bay at Pylos. The bay provided shelter and was also protected by the island of Sphacteria, which lies off the mainland, close enough to form a strait. There were no harbour facilities, although ships could be beached there, provided off-shore rocks were avoided. Once the ships were safely anchored, Demosthenes, as though to a pre-determined plan, suggested that the place could provide a useful base for control of the sea traffic to the western coast of Greece and Italy. It had good natural supplies of water and timber, always a valuable resource to a naval force, and could be made easy to defend by developing the natural defences of the bay into a fort. The plan was not received well by Demosthenes' fellow commanders, however, nor even by the individual ships' captains when he tried to interest them. The weather still remained set against any continuation of the voyage, and eventually, according to Thucydides, the soldiers with the fleet became so bored with their inactivity that they took it upon themselves to build the fortifications suggested by Demosthenes who, it might be imagined, may very well have extended his enthusiasm for the project to them. They worked very rapidly, impelled by the possibility that they might be attacked from Sparta some forty-six miles away, and in six days, had completed a fort protected from attacks from both sea and land. By then, the weather had changed, but it was agreed that the new redoubt should not be abandoned, so Demosthenes remained at Pylos with five ships while Eurymedon sailed on to Sicily with the remainder.

The Spartans were well aware of what was happening in their own backyard but initially 'made light' of the incursion, believing that a few ships and a thrown-together fort would present little threat to the finest soldiers in Greece, and besides, their major force was in Attica, undertaking the annual invasion. However, when Agis, who was commanding the invasion, heard of the events at Pylos, he was less dismissive and immediately returned from Attica and began to assemble a force to assault the Athenians by both land and sea. The Spartans concentrated on a sea-borne attack on the assumption, which was correct, that the Athenians would have fortified their position more strongly on the mainland side. They summoned some sixty ships, many from their Peloponnesian allies, and planned to block the strait between Sphacteria and the mainland by anchoring ships massed at each end, thus preventing any assistance by the Athenian fleet to their comrades on the shore at Pylos. Demosthenes, by some means, had learnt of the Spartans' imminent approach and managed to dispatch two of the five ships he still possessed to go to Eurymedon with an urgent request for the support of the remainder of the fleet.

Before the Spartans commenced their attack on the Athenians, in what they probably thought was a thoroughly professional piece of forethought, they landed four hundred and twenty picked soldiers on Sphacteria in case the Athenians attempted to utilise it in the forthcoming engagement. The Spartans then began the assault proper, sending a few ships at a time, being restricted by the narrowness of the strait and the small frontage of the fortification. They were obliged to sail up to the shore to offload their soldiers, in some cases actually running aground. Foremost amongst these was a ship commanded by the ubiquitous Brasidas, who urged his steersman to forget about protecting his vessel in his desire to get to close quarters. Even run aground, however, the ships provided for a less than effective disembarkation for the heavily armed men, who were immediately assailed by Demosthenes' troops placed on the shoreline, he having accurately predicted where they would land. The result was that the attackers were unable to form up in their accustomed ordered formations and suffered heavy casualties, including Brasidas, who received many wounds, eventually losing consciousness, and his shield, which was seized as a trophy by the Athenians. This contest went on for a day and a half before the Peloponnesian force recognised that they could make no headway and began to withdraw.

The main Athenian fleet arrived a day later and sailed into the strait without hindrance, the Peloponnesians having either forgotten their plan to block each end or withdrawn the guard ships to take part in the increasingly fruitless attack. After delaying overnight, having found that the Peloponnesian ships refused to confront them, on the next day, they resolved to attack wherever the enemy was sited, with the result that some of the enemy were captured and towed away with their crews still onshore. Others of the Peloponnesian fleet did sail out into clear water and were sunk or chased away, and at the end of the day, the Athenians were in charge of the whole of the strait, leaving the Spartan force on Sphacteria stranded under the hostile watch of the Athenian fleet.

The Spartan authorities, having received the news of the Peloponnesian force's failure, sent a commission to Pylos to review the situation. Not only had they been humiliated, with the 'finest soldiers in Greece' failing on both seas, where the Athenians had withstood a supposedly overwhelming amphibious assault, and on land, where they had been unable to overcome the 'makeshift fort,' but, worst of all, for the Spartans, their four hundred and twenty crack troops on Sphacteria had been marooned, with every likelihood of their being starved to death, or massacred by the Athenians who, with some fifty ships, would be able to muster a numerically superior force without difficulty. This concern over what might appear to be a relatively small number of men in comparison with the number of combatants involved – which would have been several thousand – might appear surprising. The explanation for this lies in the Spartans' constant obsession with their shortage of manpower due to their low birth rate and, in turn, due to their unusual marriage conventions. Married couples did not habitually live or sleep together, and the necessary activity for procreation had to be undertaken in an almost furtive manner. This shortage was the reason for their constant need to persuade their Peloponnesian neighbours to join with them in military campaigns and also to use their semi-slaves, the Helots, in warfare. In this context, the loss of four hundred and twenty of their best men would be a disaster, and the commissioners were moved to contemplate the offering of the ultimate gambit: peace, the end of the war. They agreed a truce with the Athenian commanders, which permitted them to provide rations for their stranded troops, under the inspection of the Athenians, in return for which the Peloponnesians were to deliver their ships, numbering some sixty, for the Athenians to hold as a guarantee of the observance of the truce. The Athenians were to provide transport for a Spartan embassy to Athens to discuss the terms of a peace treaty.

As was customary, the Spartan ambassadors were required to make their offer of peace to the full Athenian assembly. In Thucydides' account, the ambassadors characterised their offer of peace as permitting the Athenians the opportunity of profiting from their current advantageous position, which had arisen not from Sparta's weakness but from error. They urged that their offer should be accepted, with a recognition that it had advantages for both sides: the Athenians retaining their empire while the Spartans recovered their fellow countrymen. They counselled against any attempt to impose punitive terms, maintaining that their aim was to achieve a lasting peace enshrining friendship between the two most powerful states of Greece and suggesting that, in the absence of an agreement, when, inevitably, Athens herself suffered setbacks, the Spartans would have no compunction in taking advantage of them.

With the benefit of hindsight, it seems clear that the Spartans' proposal was a considerable climb-down. They had started the war with the express purpose of destroying the Athenian empire, which was at that point virtually unchanged, and now they were proposing to treat Athens as an equal, recognising her power and suggesting something along the lines of Kimon's idea of the two yoke-mates, with Sparta pre-eminent on land, and Athens mistress of the seas, a joint hegemony over Greece. Perhaps not surprisingly, they expected the Athenians to accept joyfully their proposal; they had, however, failed to consider the mercurial tendencies of the Athenian assembly, which at that time was very much in thrall to the demagogue Cleon, who was to play a central part in the developing situation. Cleon's view was that the Spartans had revealed their desperation at the thought of losing their stranded citizens and that they could be pushed beyond a simple termination of the war to the extent of being humiliated and required to restore historical losses to Athens. Specifically, the assembly decided that the hostages – for that was what they effectively were – must be brought as prisoners to Athens and a number of cities that the Athenians had surrendered to the Peloponnesians a decade before the war, including Nisaea, Troezen and Achaea, were to be returned to Athenian rule. These terms were obviously unacceptable to the Spartan ambassadors, and they made no response to them apart from asking that a commission of the assembly might be appointed to discuss the terms privately, probably so that their allies might not learn of the extent of their compromises. Cleon, however, 'assailed this proposal in unmeasured language,' insisting that anything that they might say should be heard by the whole city. The ambassadors, realising that the Athenians were not amenable to anything they would find acceptable, returned to Sparta.

With the Athenian rejection of the Spartans' peace proposals, the truce at Pylos was immediately terminated, and the armed stand-off was reinstated and intensified. The Athenians increased the number of their ships at the location to seventy, with constant patrols around the island, while the Peloponnesians were encamped on the shore, making frequent attacks on the fort. The Peloponnesians demanded the return of their ships, held as a guarantee of the truce, but the Athenians refused to comply, claiming with dubious justification that the truce had been broken. In the current circumstances, there was little that the Peloponnesians could do about it.

As the blockade continued, it became ever more onerous for the Athenians. Their supplies were dependent on the lengthy sea voyage from Athens, and the crews were soon suffering from shortages of food and, particularly, water. By contrast, the Spartans on the island were comparatively well supplied from the mainland by individuals tempted by large payments or, in the case of Helots, the promise of freedom, to use small boats to run the risk of capture by the Athenian patrols. Apart from their shortage of supplies, the Athenian ships had no proper anchorages nor sites to beach, so that they began to suffer the water-logging to which triremes were prone.

Eventually, the Athenian assembly became aware of the plight of the blockading force at Pylos, and inevitably, their reaction was one of anger directed against Cleon for his stand against the Spartans' offer of peace. Cleon attempted to divert their ire onto the board of generals, particularly the senior general Nicias, claiming that he should lead an expedition to capture the stranded Spartans and bring them to Athens, thus ending the need for the blockade. Nicias generally received favourable treatment in the ancient accounts, described in terms normally applicable to an aristocrat of the old school, despite his wealth being derived, like many of the 'new wealthy' in Athens, from the ownership of slaves rather than from land estates. His dignified and moderate persona contrasted with that of Cleon, who harangued the assembly with intemperate language and a deliberately outlandish appearance, trailing his *himation*, a cut-down version of the Roman toga, on the floor. Nicias' response to Cleon's attack was to suggest that if capturing the Spartans was so easy, why didn't Cleon lead an expedition himself? The board of generals would provide him with the resources he required, and he could demonstrate how it should be done. Cleon initially assumed that Nicias' suggestion was simply a ploy to deflect his criticism, and he was taken aback when it became clear that Nicias meant it seriously. (It should be pointed out that Cleon's surprise probably reflected that of many, as the command of the military resources of the state was invariably restricted to members of the board of generals, who were elected rather than being selected by lot as was the case for nearly all public officials, and Cleon had never been so elected. It must be assumed that the *Boule* had agreed this break with constitutional precedent, and perhaps this indicates the extent to which Cleon had become a thorn in the side of the administration, who were apparently prepared to accept the likely risk of a defeat if it meant being rid of him.) In his confusion, Cleon retorted that Nicias was the general, while he was simply a man of the people; however, the assembly rapidly became enthused by the idea and ever more insistently urged Cleon to accept the challenge, which after some time he did, promising either to bring the Spartan garrison back to Athens as prisoners or to kill them, within twenty days. He was asked to nominate a general to assist him, and he chose Demosthenes, who, of course, was still at Pylos. It would seem that Cleon had heard that Demosthenes was, in any case, contemplating an attack on the island and that this had, in part, at least, persuaded him to accept Nicias' challenge.

The assembly voted for the expedition, and Cleon lost little time in setting sail. He took with him, having sworn not to take regulars from the city, largely irregular forces from two of the empire's oldest allies, the island states of Lemnos and Imbros, who, for some reason, were currently stationed in Athens. Few of these were the heavily armed hoplites. Most were light-armed: *peltasts*, who threw javelins, darts and stones, and archers, numbering four hundred. Again losing little time, as Demosthenes wished to take advantage of a surge in determination on the part of the blockading force to resolve the stand-off, the two generals put into action an invasion of the island, landing troops on both sides, both facing the open sea and the mainland. In addition to the soldiers, in a departure from the normal disposition, they also landed rowers from the upper banks of some seventy ships, the *thranitai*, who probably joined the peltast groups. The tactics of the Athenians depended heavily on the 'hit and run' abilities of the light-armed troops who constantly harassed from all sides the Spartan hoplites, who were unable to pursue them effectively over the rough ground that was general over all the island. Gradually, the Spartans fell back onto the best defensive position on the island, on an outcrop of rocks on a hillside. For some time, it seemed that this might be their salvation as they were able to deploy in the standard hoplite defensive formation, of which the Spartans were past masters, and the Athenian attack was faltering. The commander of a small Messenian force (the Messenians had been the original inhabitants of the territory including Pylos), which had joined the Athenians, suggested that he could lead his men around to the rear of the Spartan position in a manner echoing the encircling that had led to the defeat of the 'Three Hundred' Spartans at Thermopylae 'to compare a smaller thing with a greater' as Thucydides remarks. After some considerable efforts, the Messenians suddenly appeared behind the Spartans, who were panicked and gave every sign of giving up resistance. Demosthenes and Cleon, realising that with the Spartans, demoralised and heavily outnumbered, were in danger of being massacred, thus losing the possibility of bringing them as prisoners and hostages to Athens. They called back their troops, therefore and offered a truce if the Spartans would surrender, to which many of them signalled that they accepted. After some difficulty in finding a senior officer on the Spartan side, as most of them had been killed, the force agreed to surrender, and they were embarked on the Athenian fleet for transport back to Athens. Of the four hundred and twenty who had been originally stationed on the island, two hundred and ninety-two survived to be brought to Athens; the Athenian casualties were negligible.

The news of the Spartan surrender was greeted with astonishment throughout Greece, where their reputation for fighting to the last man was legendary. All this, of course, augmented Cleon's newfound reputation as a military leader as he returned with the Spartan prisoners in chains within twenty days as he had promised. It was agreed that they would be kept as prisoners, as hostages against any further Peloponnesian invasion of Attica, with the threat of their execution if such occurred.

The success at Pylos was followed up by a coordinated Athenian campaign to encircle the Peloponnese. The fort at Pylos was maintained, with additional reinforcements from Messenians and some Helots. The Spartans attempted to negotiate an Athenian withdrawal but were unable to offer anything to tempt Athens to give up this strategically important toehold, which seemed to be resistant to any attempt to overrun it. The Athenians then took control of the island of Cythera, at the southeastern extremity of the Peloponnese, which had been garrisoned by the Spartans but which fell to a force of sixty ships and two thousand hoplites under the command of Nicias. This gave them a base for attacking the eastern coast of Laconia (the area of the Peloponnese surrounding Sparta itself), using the hit-and-run tactics that they had developed. These continual attacks and occupations had a demoralising effect on the Spartans, who attempted to counter them by establishing garrisons in coastal areas, but which, given their limited numbers, meant that these resources were thinly spread and were frequently obliged to retreat to fortifications when Athenian raiding parties landed rather than offering significant resistance.

Eventually, an opportunity to ease the Athenian stranglehold on the Peloponnese presented itself in the form of an invitation by the inhabitants of Chalcidice, a territory on the north eastern Aegean, for the Spartans to send an army to protect the Chalcidians when, as they intended, they revolted from Athenian rule. The Spartans, with perhaps uncharacteristic eagerness, were happy to fall in with this request, seeing it as providing a 'second front' to divert at least some of the Athenians' forces. Accordingly, they sent a force of some two thousand under the command of Brasidas, now well established as their leading general, northwards on the land journey to Chalcidice – the Spartans still having no operative troop-carrying fleet. Brasidas had reached Corinth when he learnt of the Athenians' latest annual attack on nearby Megara and took immediate steps to confront it, most significantly sending an urgent request for support to the Boeotians, Athens' traditional enemies, who responded rapidly with two thousand hoplites and six hundred horse. The Athenians were preparing to enter Megara, having fully invested the city's port of Nisaea, where they maintained a garrison, and also breaking down the long walls connecting the port to the city that they themselves had built. On learning of Brasidas' presence and the size of his forces, they retired into Nisaea and awaited his next move. Brasidas moved his troops to a defensive position outside Megara and sent the cavalry towards Nisaea, where it was engaged by the Athenian cavalry. The action resulted in no clear advantage to either side, although the commander of the Boeotion cavalry was killed with a number of his men. The Athenians recognised that they were significantly outnumbered and, after considering that most of their objective had been achieved, decided that there was little to be gained and the possibility of serious losses by a full-scale assault, and they quietly withdrew. On seeing this, Brasidas dismissed his allies and resumed his journey to Chalcidice, having supported an oligarchic takeover in Megara. From this episode, he derived a propaganda advantage in being able to claim that the Athenians had refused to face him, which was literally true, although he had made no attempt to make them commit their full forces to an attack.

The major part of the territory through which he had to travel was Thessaly. The Thessalians were generally friendly towards Athens and, in any case, were unlikely to welcome a sizeable body of heavy-armed alien soldiers. Brasidas was provided with an escort by some of the local Spartan sympathisers to guide his journey, but he was brought up short by another group who met him to object to his presence and demand that he turnabout and leave Thessaly. Brasidas' response was to give an undertaking that if the Thessalians objected to his travelling through their territory, he would abandon his journey, and the opposing group left, presumably to gather more like-minded fellow citizens. On the advice of his escort, he pressed ahead, with all speed and without stopping, to reach the Thessalian border before an effective opposition could be organised.

The next stage of the journey was through Macedonia, whose king, Perdiccas, was not particularly anti-Athenian, but who welcomed Brasidas and his force as possible allies in a local conflict in which he was engaged. As he offered to pay half of the wages of Brasidas' men and to join with him in encouraging the secession of various states from Athenian rule, Brasidas was happy to agree. The augmented army then continued to Chalcidice.

The first target for detachment from Athens was the city of Acanthus on the peninsula of Acte, to the southeast of Chalcidice. The Acanthians had disagreed with the Chalcidians and refused to admit Brasidas' force. Brasidas requested that he might enter the city alone and address its citizens, and this request was granted. Brasidas' speech exemplified the Spartan approach, with a velvet glove containing an iron fist. He began by expressing disappointment that he and his army had not been welcomed with the joy that he had anticipated as being the natural response to the bringing of liberty to a city oppressed by the rapacious Athenians. He reminded them that the Spartans had entered the war for this very purpose of 'freeing the Hellenes,' and now this promise was being honoured. He apologised for the delay in coming to their rescue but explained that Athenian hostility had necessitated extensive and time-consuming defensive operations. He then moved on to question whether the Acanthians were afraid of liberty when so many other states were throwing off the Athenian yoke. The tone then hardened considerably in his suggesting that those who refused to choose liberty might well have it forced upon them. Finally came a straightforward threat: he was not prepared to see the noble work of freeing the Hellenes compromised by a recalcitrant state that, by remaining subject to Athens, was helping the Athenians in the war by their tribute payments to them. If this were to be the case, he would ravage the Acanthian's country 'without scruple,' and he urged them to choose liberty for the glory of their city and the protection of their property. Not surprisingly, when the Acanthians debated amongst themselves, they agreed to accept Brasidas' force and secede from Athens.

Next, Brasidas turned his attention further east to Amphipolis, a city on the river Strymon, not far inland from the Aegean. This area, close to the island of Thasos, had been a focus of Athenian interest and colonisation since the days of Peisistratos and was valuable both for its gold mines and its strategic position. Amphipolis had been constructed by the Athenians and was regarded as a key subject of the empire. Its population was a mixture of peoples, with a few Athenians, Ionian Greeks and 'barbarians' of various descriptions. Perhaps unsurprisingly, it contained a faction who were well-disposed to Brasidas, and the idea of seceding, and a message was sent to him promising to open the city gates if his army approached. Brasidas accordingly marched to the outskirts of the city, having crossed the Strymon over the nearby bridge, which had been only lightly guarded. He waited for the gates to be opened, but the conspirators had been detected and caught in the act of trying to carry out their promise, and so the city remained protected. Instead of attempting to take the city by assault, which would probably have been fairly easy as the defensive forces were meagre, he allowed his troops to plunder the properties outside the walls. This delay gave the Athenian general stationed in Amphipolis time to send for help to the other Athenian general in the area, who was Thucydides, later to become the historian of the war. Thucydides was stationed at Thasos with seven ships, and he set out immediately to sail to Amphipolis.

Possibly getting wind of the Athenian reinforcements, on the next day, Brasidas made a more determined effort to enter the city, and by the time Thucydides reached Eion, the port town at the mouth of the Strymon, he had taken control of Amphipolis. Brasidas sent a force to overcome Eion and complete his mastery of the area, but Thucydides was able to organise the local defences, and his attempt was repulsed. The Athenians were 'seriously alarmed' at the loss of Amphipolis, which supplied a useful tribute and was also a major source of timber for shipbuilding. Strategically, the city commanded the easterly land route to many more Athenian subject cities by virtue of its proximity to the Strymon bridge, which was the only crossing giving easy access as the river was fed by a large lake from the North; it was also close to valuable gold mines. Thucydides' failure to reach the city in time to prevent its capitulation was punished by the Athenian assembly with an exile of twenty years. He comments philosophically on this, saying that it enabled him to observe the war and gather evidence from all sides of the conflict, and so it is to this military setback that his invaluable record has been made available to posterity.

Brasidas' success at Amphipolis encouraged several of Athens' subject allies to secede from her control, sending solicitations to him to, as they saw it, free them, having been persuaded by his standard rhetoric and reputation for fairness to those at least who 'chose liberty.' They also believed that the Athenians' power was waning, reinforced in this by Brasidas' other piece of propaganda: the questionable claim that they had refused to confront him at Nisaea. He continued his campaign with an attack on the city of Torone, lying in the centre of the three promontories protruding from the south of Chalcidice. As usual, he was assisted by a conspiracy in the city to open the gate to his forces and was able to take control before most of the citizens and the Athenian garrison became aware of his presence. A number of the garrison escaped to the fort of Lecythos close by, together with some of the citizens who remained loyal to the Athenians. Brasidas called a meeting of the citizens and rehearsed his message, inviting them to choose liberty and also to urge that the conspirators amongst them should be honoured as having enabled this opportunity to be presented to them. The citizens acquiesced, and Brasidas promised that those who had sided with the Athenians would not suffer. They would come to recognise the superior qualities of the Spartans and be friendly to them. He also demanded that the Athenians should depart under a flag of truce from their fort, but they rejected this. Eventually, he attacked the fort and, after some resistance, overran it, putting to death everyone he found there. Those who escaped were taken off in Athenian warships, which sailed to Pallene on the westmost promontory.

Brasidas, understandably, was ambitious to widen the scope of his exploits and sent word to Sparta asking for reinforcements, but this request was ignored. The reasons for this seem to have been a combination of jealousy of his success on the part of some in Sparta and the persistent obsession with those captured at Sphacteria, still held prisoner in Athens, which had inspired a desire to end hostilities rather than intensify them. In line with this, they pressed for a year's truce with the Athenians, feeling that having experienced their recent setbacks, they would be amenable both to a truce but also to negotiating an end to the war and the release of their men. As the Spartans had assumed, the Athenians were only too willing to have some respite from Brasidas' erosion of their empire, and the truce was agreed.

Before the news of the truce had reached Chalcidice, another Athenian subject ally, Scione, situated on the Pallene promontory, revolted against imperial rule. Brasidas moved quickly to take advantage of this new opportunity. He was greeted with something approaching hero-worship by the Scionians, who showered him with honours and a golden crown. Brasidas then intended to consolidate his hold on the Pallene peninsula by moving on Mende and Potidea, both of which were under Athenian rule. His plans were interrupted, however, by the arrival in the area of the ship carrying Athenian and Spartan ambassadors bringing the news of the truce. On hearing of the revolt of Scione, the Athenian ambassador investigated the date on which it had occurred and concluded that this was two days after the truce was declared, and thus, Brasidas' take-over was in breach of the agreement. Brasidas, however, refused to give up Scione, understandably causing great anger in Athens. The Athenian assembly carried a resolution moved, inevitably, by Cleon to send a punitive expedition to re-take Scione and deal harshly with its inhabitants.

Further salt was applied to the wound when Mende also revolted and again was visited by Brasidas and added to the list of states having chosen the liberty of Spartan rule despite the truce. The rage of the Athenians was thus further intensified, and the disciplining of Mende added to the objectives of the punitive expedition. Eventually, a force was sent under the command of Nicias, the senior general, and with some difficulty, Athenian rule was re-imposed on both Scione and Mende. Following these interruptions, the truce was respected until its termination as originally agreed.

When the truce expired in 422 BC, the Athenians, who felt keenly the loss of Amphipolis, agreed to Cleon's proposal that he lead an expedition to re-take the city. The force involved was of a significant size, with thirty ships carrying twelve hundred Athenian hoplites and three hundred horsemen, together with 'numerous allies'; there was, however, a suggestion that these forces were less than convinced of Cleon's qualities as a military leader, despite his success at Pylos. The force sailed first to Torone, the important city on the central of the three peninsulae south of the Chalcidice mainland, which Brasidas had used as his base. Fortunately for Cleon, Brasidas was away at the time, and the Spartan left in charge was caught napping by the marauding fleet, and the city was restored to Athenian control. Leaving a garrison there, Cleon then sailed to the port town of Eion, at the mouth of the Strymon, south of Amphipolis, where he landed his troops and sent requests to allies for reinforcements, hoping to overrun Amphipolis rapidly rather than having to undertake a lengthy siege. He then intended to wait for these reinforcements to arrive. At the same time, Brasidas, who had heard of the attack on Torone and had set out to intervene, only to abandon the idea of hearing that the city had fallen to the Athenians, then marched to Amphipolis, correctly assuming that this would be the next target.

Cleon's plan to wait quietly for reinforcements was soon undermined by the dissatisfaction of his troops, who had been fired up by their success at Torone and were 'disgusted' at what they took to be the lack of spirit on the part of their commander. Cleon was thus persuaded to move his troops up to Amphipolis in a half-hearted and half-thought-out manoeuvre essentially to reconnoitre the disposition of whatever enemy force there was. Prefiguring the Grand Old Duke of York by some two millennia, he marched his troops up to the top of a hill overlooking the city, apparently ready to march them down again on the first sign of any serious opposition. Meanwhile, Brasidas had a sizeable force within the city but made no immediate move to come out; indeed, he was careful to avoid any great show of activity. He observed the Athenian force from the walls and recognised their lack of urgency and organisation, and told his troops that the enemy was already mentally defeated. He divided them into two: a small group of one hundred and fifty to act as 'shock troops' and the rest to wait for the command to join him. Cleon had joined a scouting party which had approached the city when he received a report from further forward that, in fact, there was a considerable force within the city. He decided immediately to order a retreat, which his troops began to obey in a fairly well-organised manner, wheeling around and thus presenting their flank to the watching Brasidas, who ordered his crack troops out of the nearest gate to attack them, panicking those who received the assault directly and were caught unawares. On seeing the success of this initial action, he ordered the remainder of his force to join the fight, and eventually, the entire Athenian force was put to flight. Cleon was killed while fleeing, but also, much against the prevailing run of the contest, Brasidas was severely wounded, and though surviving to be carried back into the city and learning that his force had triumphed, he died. The survivors of the Athenian force, which had sustained the loss of some six hundred men, straggled back to Eion, where they were embarked, and the fleet sailed for home carrying the news of this latest and most severe setback.

At the end of the summer of 422 BC, the Spartans assembled a force of some nine hundred to reinforce their garrison at Amphipolis. The general in charge, Rhamphias, attempted to follow Brasidas' route through Thessaly, but this time, the Thessalians were not caught by surprise and refused to let the Spartans through their territory. Faced with this and with the knowledge of Brasidas' death, they called off the expedition and returned home. Their decision also reflected the Spartans' increasing desire for peace, still motivated by the obsession with obtaining the release of those captured at Sphacteria and imprisoned in Athens. At the same time, with the death of Cleon, the Athenians had lost the main protagonist of the war, and the string of reverses culminating in the loss of Amphipolis had engendered a disillusionment with it in the assembly. The time was ripe, therefore, for negotiating peace, and the process was activated by two individuals with strong interests in achieving it: Pleistoanax, a Spartan king, and Nicias, the senior Athenian general.

Pleistoanax was the king who had abandoned his foray into Attica some nineteen years before and had been accused of being bribed to do so and banished. After years of somewhat suspiciously frequent admonitions by the oracle of Delphi that the Spartans should release him from his banishment, he was eventually allowed to return, with his regal state, but was still regarded in a poor light by many. He felt that by seizing the opportunity of obtaining peace and the recovery of the captives, he would improve his standing with his subjects. Nicias enjoyed the quality of the generalship recommended by Napoleon – that of being lucky. Despite being involved in numerous actions, he had avoided any of the disasters that the Athenians had suffered, and he was keen to see the war ended and, with it, the possibility that his unblemished record might be tarnished. The negotiations leading to the peace treaty were lengthy, and even after it was signed, it was immediately repudiated by some of Sparta's allies. And there were many in the Athenian assembly who voiced objections and recalled with bitterness the rejection of the Spartan offer of peace after the capture of the marooned force at Sphacteria. The most significant features of the treaty were, for the Spartans, the release of the prisoners held at Athens and the evacuation of the Athenian force at Pylos, and for the Athenians, the return of Amphipolis and the retention of some of their conquests, such as Nisaea. The Athenians were prompt in their release of the prisoners, but the Spartan governor of Amphipolis refused to give up his control of the city, claiming the Chalcidians generally disagreed with the terms of the treaty and that he would not act against the wishes of the people. This, of course, was received with outrage by the Athenians, who now regretted having given up the hostages so promptly and were firmly set against giving up their Laconian foothold at Pylos. Negotiations continued, leading to another treaty which established Sparta and Athens as allies and which was even less respected than the first. And so this uneasy peace, the 'Peace of Nicias,' which was supposed to last for fifty years, drifted on for a short time, with many breaches and dissatisfaction on both sides. Neither Amphipolis nor Pylos were given up.

Chapter 7
The Old Oligarch

At this juncture, we break off what has been essentially a diachronic narrative, to concentrate briefly on the single, distinctly flawed work of an unknown author. The work is known by the title *The Constitution of the Athenians,* and its author is generally referred to, in the Anglosphere at least, as the *Old Oligarch*. In other locations, the author is given as Pseudo-Xenophon, or the work is simply described as 'attributed to Xenophon,' as the result of what is now generally regarded as a mistaken inclusion of it by ancient editors in the corpus of the Athenian soldier and historian Xenophon.

As suggested above, the work is flawed in many aspects; it is repetitious, exaggerated, disjointed and inconsistent, and the obvious question arises: why bother with it? The answer is that despite all these faults, it provides a fascinating glimpse of what the Athenian upper class, the oligarchs, or at least some of them, thought of the radical democracy under whose rule they lived. What is even more significant for this book is the surprising fact that, despite the author's deprecating attitude to democracy, he recognises that the wealth and security of the Athens of his day was heavily dependent on the *demos* – the poor, the 'worthless' *thetes* – because *they manned the ships of the fleet,* which was the mainstay of the empire, and so he maintains that they deserved their pre-eminence in the government. In this, he was unique amongst contemporary and near-contemporary authors. Thucydides eloquently describes the advantages of naval power but is distinctly unenthusiastic about democracy. Plato and Aristotle are both anti-democratic and specifically downplay the importance of the navy precisely because it is so closely associated with democracy. Aristotle goes so far as to belittle the significance of Salamis and also to suggest that the only naval personnel worthy of any respect were the marines, who generally came from the 'hoplite class.' Aristotle's term for naval crews, in general, was *ochlos nautikos* – the 'naval mob,' and he suggests that there is no need for those manning the fleet to be citizens. Xenophon – the real one – despite being an Athenian, was a 'laconiser,' an admirer of Sparta, and an anti-democrat, fought against Athenian democratic forces in 404 BC and joined the Spartan army under King Agesilaus in his Ionian campaign at the beginning of the 4th century. He occasionally mentions naval affairs but is uninterested in their political significance.

It is perhaps no surprise to discover that the name, Old Oligarch, is currently generally regarded as not only misleading but straightforwardly wrong in that the work reflects anything but a mature command of style and content and is clearly a juvenile effort, with many of the hallmarks of a paper put together probably for public discussion under the tutelage of a sophist, or professional philosopher and teacher. The sophists, amongst whom, despite his undoubted objection to the term, was included Socrates, were proud of their ability to argue in equally convincing ways both for and against any proposition, and the gravamen underlying the paper is a typically sophistic argument by which the author, having made clear his disapproval of the democratic regime in Athens, sets out to show that the many objectionable characteristics of this democracy are in fact necessary to ensure its continued existence and that the *demos*, despite their general ignorance and lawlessness, are quite aware of this and will resist any attempt to modify them to their own disadvantage. It might be conjectured that the apparent cynicism underlying this argument persuaded readers in earlier times of the maturity, not to say the worldliness of the author, hence the 'Old,' but the stylistic shortcomings noted previously make this highly unlikely. Oligarch he (almost) certainly was, but old he was not. In the remainder of this section, the Old Oligarch will be referred to as 'X.'

It is conjectured then that X was a young man from a wealthy Athenian family who was undergoing an advanced education under the supervision of one of the many peripatetic philosopher-teachers, or sophists ('wise men') who plied their trade in Classical Athens. The term trade is introduced because of the undoubted financial implications of sophistic training – sophists did not bestow their pearls of wisdom for nothing – and the fact that X was receiving such an education is evidence of his wealthy background, confirmed by his (nuanced) oligarchic outlook.

A further controversy surrounding X's work concerns the date when it was written. Most of the treatise is expressed in generalities, with very few references to historical events that might be used to fix the date of its creation with a reasonable degree of certainty. This is not the place to examine the numerous competing suggestions that have and are still being made. This discussion accepts the conjecture that the work was written at what might be regarded as the apogee of the Athenians' campaign during the Archidamian war, shortly after their victory at Sphacteria, which was significant for this book in that it was a victory of an Athenian naval force over a Spartan infantry unit, during which the *thranitai* – the rowers who manned the upper rank of oars, who are generally thought to have been Athenians – were pressed into service as ground troops. The relevant date is around 424 BC.

X begins his treatise in exemplary fashion, providing an introduction that encapsulates much of his argument and lays out a programme for its development: "But with regard to the Athenians' constitution, I do not approve of the fact that they have chosen to have this type of constitution, for the following reason, that in making their choice they have chosen that the worthless men should do better than the valuable… However, given that they have decided that things should be as they are, I shall demonstrate how effectively they preserve their constitution and also transact their other public business, in those respects in those respects in which the rest of the Greeks think that they act mistakenly."

X immediately strikes a controversial note in respect of the just deserts of the *demos* arising from their naval service: "First of all, I will say this, that the poor and the *demos* are justified there [i.e. in Athens] in having more than the well-born and the rich, because of the fact that it is the *demos* who sail the ships and who confer its strength on the city... much more than the hoplites and the well-born and the valuable." This (abbreviated) sentence contains so much that is revolutionary that it is almost impossible to do it justice in a relatively brief summary. The idea that the poor, to use the least value-loaded term for the lowest class, as compared with *poneroi* – the 'worthless' as used in the first paragraph, with its well-understood equivalent *demos*, the 'people,' again signifying both poverty and moral debasement, should 'have more' than the hoplites and the 'valuable' – the *chrestoi* – would have been either laughable or akin to heresy to the typical oligarch. The mention of the hoplites is particularly noteworthy. As noted previously (Chapter 1), the hoplites were mainly drawn from the *zeugitai*. Generally farmers with small land holdings, and as such, were the second to the lowest class of citizen. However, the image of the hoplite, a heavily-armed infantryman, standing unyielding with his comrades in the phalanx as they withstood the onrushing waves of the enemy was central to contemporary Athenian perceptions of military valour and *arete* (honour and general excellence). And this value structure was not restricted to Athens but was certainly ascribed to Sparta and other Greek states. The fact that the Athenian empire was built on naval supremacy and the correspondingly heroic actions of trireme crews was virtually never overtly recognised in literature, apart from a few mentions in Aristophanes or any of the many monuments created in the classical era, and so X's declaration represents a significant counter-cultural gesture.

It might be argued that X's declaration is so counter-cultural as to cast some doubt on the theory that his work is an academic discussion paper in that it was not necessary to downplay the contribution of the iconic hoplite in order to justify the emancipation of the demos and that he might be, very successfully, hiding a demotic sympathy behind the anti-democratic persona – a double-bluff in fact. It is also interesting that X displays a knowledge of the names of the various roles of the members of a trireme crew, which is surprisingly detailed for one with his assumed background. He gives these as 'the steersmen, the boatswains, the lieutenants, the look-outs and the shipwrights.' These, with the exception of the steersmen, who were effectively captains, were referred to as the *hyperesia*, usually translated as 'petty officers.' Significantly, although there is considerable debate about whether the rowers of the ships were Athenians, with current views tending to support the idea that many were probably not, there is much more agreement that the steersmen and *hyperesia* were generally Athenian citizens. X does not include rowers in his list, although the term translated as 'sail' in 'it is the *demos* who sail the ships' could also mean 'row.' This suggests again that X was more knowledgeable about naval matters than might be expected of a young oligarch.

The somewhat vague characterisation of the *demos*' advantages as 'having more than the well-born and the rich' is clarified in the next sentence: "Since this is the case [i.e., that the *demos* confers its strength on the city], it seems right that everyone should share in the holding of public office, both the allotted and the elective offices, and that any citizen who wishes should be allowed to have his say [i.e., in the *ekklesia*]." What is certainly clear is that 'having more' did not mean possessing greater or even comparable wealth than the well-born and rich. The huge disparity of material wealth between rich and poor in Athens continued well beyond the collapse of the democratic regime: the lot of the *thetes* and the poor tradesmen may well have been ameliorated by the economic benefits of the empire, but this would have been measured in obols per day (an obol being one-sixth of a drachma – one drachma being the standard daily rate of pay for a workman for much of the fifth century) when the rich would typically enjoy an annual income measured in Talents, a Talent being six thousand drachmai. The wealth that democracy did bestow on the poor citizens, and only on citizens, was political wealth – in X's words, 'Any citizen who wishes is allowed to have his say.'

X then resiles somewhat from his assertion that the demos held all the public offices by admitting that: "there are offices which bring safety to the whole *demos* when well conducted, but danger when not well conducted, and the *demos* do not want any share in these (for example they do not think they should have an allotted share in the generalships or the cavalry commands])." X uses demos here with two meanings. In the first instance, 'whole *demos*' means the entire Athenian populace, rich and poor. In the second *demos* is back to meaning the poor, the worthless. X claims that these offices critical to the safety of the polis are unpaid, which was probably true for most of the fifth century and therefore was not desired by the poor, who were interested only in public offices that offered receipt of pay and domestic benefit – a telling insight into X's personal view. There were two reasons why 'the poor' did not desire unpaid public offices, one of which X was undoubtedly aware of, the other probably beyond his comprehension. The first is that the board of generals, ten in number, one from each tribe, was subject to an annual election, but unlike other public offices, there was no bar to a general serving for several consecutive years – indeed, the Athenian citizenry seemed to have adopted the sensible view that successful generals should be maintained in their position. Notably, Pericles was elected general for many years. Unsurprisingly, generals were often drawn from dynastic families, which inevitably were firmly established in the upper class. It was not until the fourth century that a general who had come from a relatively poor background, Iphikrates, was elected. (The election of the demagogue Cleon to the generalship is sometimes mentioned as an exception to the exclusive hold over the generalship by the upper class, but, although not a member of the landed rich and having the posthumous reputation as a 'man of the people,' Cleon was certainly well-off.) The second reason was, of course, that the poor needed to earn a living, which required full-time commitment, and so they were only able to enter public office if they were paid enough for themselves and their families to live on. The payment of public officials was one of the pillars of democracy for this reason.

X continues the development of his contemptuous attitude to the poor in the subsequent section by providing an explanation for "a thing which some people are surprised at, namely the fact that in every area they assign more to the worthless and the poor and the common people than they do to the valuable." Neglecting the vagueness of the 'more' that is assigned, his explanation is that "it is precisely through this practice that they preserve their democracy. For the common people and the inferior classes will increase the strength of their democracy by doing well and by increasing the numbers of themselves and their like. If, however, the rich and valuable do well, the common people make the opposition to themselves strong."

It is clear from this that the idea of social mobility is entirely alien to X. The thought that some members of the poor might, with the advantages which X claims are showered upon them, achieve a level of wealth where they were no longer poor and thus no longer subject to the inexorable process by which "poverty tends to lead... into shameful behaviour" (1.5) is simply outside his conception. X makes this clear in an earlier paragraph in which he essentially divides humanity, not only in Athens or Greece, into two races – the rich and the poor –

separated both by an exclusively different moral and political outlook and, significantly, hostile opposition: "Throughout the world, the best element is opposed to democracy. For within the best of men, there is the least amount of licentiousness and injustice... whereas within the *demos* there is the greatest ignorance, indiscipline and worthlessness."

X then extends his binary view of humanity into a consideration of how this affects the systems of government espoused by, on the one hand, the *demos*, on the other, the 'valuable.' Taking the *demos* first – "they do not wish the state to be well governed while they themselves are slaves, but rather to be free and rule... the *demos* actually derive their strength and their freedom precisely from what you consider not to be good government." Turning to the *chrestoi* – the 'valuable': "If you are looking for good government, you will find that; first, the cleverest men draw up the laws for them. After that, the valuable men will punish the worthless ones... and they will not allow wild persons to be members of the Council or to speak or to attend meetings of the assembly. So, as a result of these good measures, the demos would very quickly be reduced to slavery." The term *douleian*, translated here as slavery, implies loss of political rights, as, for example, applied to the subject allies of the empire, rather than actual subjugation. X here makes a remarkably prescient prefiguring of what actually occurred in the oligarchic revolt of 411 BC when the democratic government was overthrown and replaced by the rule of the Four Hundred – being four hundred of the 'best men'

– who devised a constitution falsely claimed to be based on 'the constitution of our forefathers,' which removed the Boule and the political rights of any citizen not qualifying as one of the richest three thousand. A similar reduction of the *demos* to slavery was effected after the end of the Peloponnesian war by the puppet oligarchic government installed by the Spartan general Lysander, known as the 'Thirty Tyrants,' who, however, did not attempt to justify their actions by a new constitution.

These apparent confirmations of X's antagonistic bifurcated society are, however, exceptions that prove only that, as might be expected, Athenian society, which exhibited such a colossal range of inequality, contained a probably widely fluctuating minority that was genuinely anti-democratic. On the other hand, it cannot have escaped X's notice, as a well-educated young man, that the democracy that he so deplored owed its existence to a number of individuals – Kleisthenes, Themistocles, Aristides, Ephialtes and Pericles, who were all very wealthy men, and certainly 'valuable, useful' etc. Certainly, Pericles, who was responsible for the most radical developments that completed the democracy that was in power when X was writing, was a large-scale land owner and was connected (unhappily) by marriage to the Alcmaeonids: probably the foremost family in Athens after their rehabilitation at the beginning of the fifth century. The picture of a homogeneous oligarchy defined by its opposition to democracy is obviously false.

Turning to the other side of the binary divide, the logical outcome of the *demos*' "increasing the strength of their democracy" to the disadvantage of the valuable would surely be to amplify the exactions made on them until equality of wealth is achieved throughout the state. A number of states, notably including Corinth, in close proximity to Athens, had seen civil strife, or *stasis*, where the poor had risen against the wealthy and extirpated many of them. By contrast, the impositions made on the Athenian rich, as described by X, are restricted to the undertaking of liturgies, the enforced financial support of activities deemed valuable by the state. "In the case of public choral performances and athletic competitions and trireme provision, they know that the rich provide the choruses while the demos take part in them... while the demos take part in trireme service... Thus, the demos think they have a right to receive money for singing and dancing and sailing in the ships, so as to get wealth for themselves and to make the rich poorer." As X says, the liturgies included support of some one hundred festivals a year, with costs to the *leitourgoi* ranging from 300 drachmai to several Talents, but by far the most demanding liturgy and the one with critical significance for the Athenian state and its empire was that of the *trierarchy*, whereby the running costs of each trireme on active service in the fleet was underwritten for one year by a trierarch, who was also required to sail with 'his' ship during its actions during the period. The trierarch did not pay for the construction of the ship nor the wages of the crew, both of which were paid from state funds, but was responsible for its outfitting and any additional costs during the ship's service. Although not responsible for the basic wage of the crew, he would often have to provide additional money for rations, which had to be purchased during the voyages as the restricted space on a trireme did not permit the carrying of extensive stores.

The *leitourgoi* who undertook the liturgies were the richest men in the state, and during the Archidamian war (431 – 422), there were some 300 or 400 trierarchs who were called upon to perform this particular liturgy, amounting to about one percent of the male citizen population. The amount of expenditure varied widely, with the main determining factor being the state of the trireme in each case when it was returned to the state shipyards at the Piraeus at the end of the trierarch's year of service. The cost of returning the ship to a battle-ready state was born by the trierarch in question, and this could be avoided only if any damage was caused by enemy action or unusually severe weather. In a number of cases where a ship was lost by incompetence, the trierarch was liable to pay for the entire building of a replacement. X's assertion that the liturgies, and the trierarchy in particular, were devised by the poor to enrich themselves and impoverish the rich is, as remarked by Marr and Rhodes, absurd. The pay for the rowers ranged from one-half (3 obols) to one drachma a day, which was a living wage, although hardly princely, and one-half was often paid in arrears at the end of a period of service to discourage desertion. The costs to a trierarch could be considerable, in the number of Talents, but these men were extremely rich, and there is evidence that at least some of them accepted that the trierarchy provided a vehicle for the display of their wealth in a manner that earned them *charis*, or the gratitude of their fellow citizens, which could be valuable when they, as not infrequently happened, were subject to accusations in the law courts. The element of risk to a trierarch as he sailed in 'his' ship was quite real – many trierarchs lost their lives during various expeditions – and this also provided the opportunity for bravery in the military context that had been a defining characteristic of the aristocracy, and which the paucity of infantry warfare during the period had restricted. The possibility of the impoverishment of trirarchs during the fifth century, until 4013 or thereabouts, was remote. Even so, there were regulations and procedures to prevent this. No trierarch was required to perform the liturgy for two years in succession (later three), although some elected to do so. If a man nominated for the trierarchy felt that he could not afford it, he could avoid the liturgy by identifying someone wealthier to undertake it by a process known as *antidosis*. If the proposed substitute declined the liturgy, the case would be taken to court to determine whether he actually was wealthier and if it was so determined, he was obliged either to assume the responsibility or to exchange his estate with that of the original nominee. This apparently somewhat cumbersome procedure appears to have worked quite well; the 4th-century orator Demosthenes was obliged to undertake a triarchy as the result of a claim of *antidosis*. Thus, the notion that the trierarchy was deliberately designed to impoverish the rich was a symptom of X's view of the binary class struggle as a zero-sum game.

In the later stages of the first part of X's treatise, he turns to the attitude of the *demos* to Athens' allies – the members of the Delian League – now, with few exceptions, tribute-paying subjects of the Empire. X maintains that the forces of the democratic regime 'sail out… and bring malicious charges against, and hate, the valuable among them.' This is X's version of the practice, described in Chapter 3, of Athens keeping a watchful eye on political activities in the allies' territories, ready to nip any anti-Athens movements in the bud by arresting the ringleaders and putting them on trial in Athens. X generalises this to suggest that the criterion for such a process is simply being 'valuable,' i.e., one of the *chrestoi*, while ignoring the reality that the objective was to root out sedition. It is true that almost invariably those fermenting anti-Athenian sentiment would be oligarchs – the 'valuable' – but on the whole, the Athenians left those who displayed no objection to Athenian rule free of 'malicious charges.' X justifies his assertion of the demos' generalised hatred of the allied 'valuable' by claiming that 'if the rich and strong come into power in the allied states, the empire of the Athenian demos will only last for a very short time.' In order to forestall this supposedly inexorable outcome, X claims that consistent with their overriding pursuit of self-survival, the demos 'take away the political rights of the valuable, and confiscate their property and exile and kill them,' then reverting to the binary, zero-sum class struggle, this time in the Allies' societies, he adds 'and, correspondingly promote the interests of the worthless.'

While there is no evidence that the Athenians adopted a general policy of ruthless suppression of the oligarchic sections of the allies' societies, it is true that when, as in Lesbos in 428, there was a revolt led by the oligarchy ruling Mytilene against Athenian rule, the Athenian response was robust, as described in Chapter 3.

Although there is no proof, it does not seem beyond the realms of possibility that X was aware not only of the events at Mityline but also of the denouement and the arguments put forward in the ekklesia. Accepting this, it can be seen that his depiction of the attitude of the Athenian demos to their allies is a typical exaggeration of an extreme example of the exercise of imperial power. Thus, it is true that Mitylinaean landowners lost their property and were obliged to rent it back from the Athenian Cleruchs to whom it had been given. However, they, with the exception of the thousand or so ringleaders of the revolt, were not killed nor apparently exiled. It should also be recognised that the Mitylinaean revolt was, as Cleon remarked, peculiarly offensive to the Athenians. The Mitylinaeans had enjoyed a privileged status as an ally, one shared only by Chios, in that they did not pay tribute, probably as a result of their possession of a sizeable navy, which they placed at the disposal of Athens on occasion. Their motivation for the revolt was their apparent fear that they would be 'enslaved' like the subject allies, despite the fact that the Athenians had never given them any reason to believe this.

Although X's characterisation of the Athenian demos' attitude to the 'valuable' of their allies is an exaggeration of an extreme case, it cannot be denied that it contains elements of reality. The establishment of cleruchies in misbehaving states inevitably punished the rich landowners by the confiscation of their land, while the demos were largely unaffected. And his assertion that the oppression of the oligarchs would 'promote the interests of the worthless' echoes Diodotus' claim that the allies' *demoi* would support the Athenians. Towards the end of his treatise, X returns to Athenian foreign policy: "Also the Athenians are thought to have a mistaken policy, in that they take the side of the inferior classes in states which are involved in civil war." Again, X answers this with a typical piece of realpolitik: "But they do this with good reason. If they took the side of the better classes, they would be supporting those who do not have the same views as themselves." And he then returns to his binary worldview: "For in no state is the best element well-disposed to the *demos*; rather in every state it is the worst element which is well disposed to the *demos*. For like is well disposed to like. That is why the Athenians choose to support the side which is related to themselves." In its negative way, this agrees with Diodotus' argument.

In the second part of X's treatise, he expatiates on the advantages of naval power, coming to the subject rather abruptly following an admission that the Athenians' hoplite force is not their 'strong point,' but claiming that this is quite intentional in that all that is required is for the Athenians to be stronger than their individual allies. (This rather casual indifference to the supposed inferiority of Athens' hoplites echoes the sentiment of the first paragraph and, as remarked previously, contrasts markedly with what most sources suggest was the current imaginary of military prowess, particularly when compared with sea-based forces.) He then gives the justification for this, which is that the allies are generally isolated, "as many are islanders" and thus "unable to unite their cities into a single unit," unlike "those who are subjects on land," who are able to so unite "and fight all together" presumably against an imperial oppressor. X skates over the fact that some of Athens' subjects are situated on the mainland by maintaining that the need to "import or export something" will make them compliant with the 'rulers of the sea,' a phrase that appears frequently in the ensuing sections.

The rulers of the sea possess many advantages, according to X, all of which emphasize the dependence of the city on its navy and the *ochlos nautikos* that mans it, as follows:

1. They have the ability to do what the rulers of the land are able to do only sometimes – "namely, to ravage the territory of the more powerful. For it is possible for them to sail along the coast and put in where there is no enemy, or where there are only a few, and then if enemy forces do attack, to re-embark and sail away." This is an accurate description of the policy adopted by the Athenians in the early days of the Archidamian War when they staged a number of 'hit and run' raids on Lacedaemon. It is also a form of warfare deprecated by Plato in *Laws*, Book IV, where he maintains that the ability to flee inculcates cowardice in the attacking force.

2. "They have the ability to sail far away from their own country, whereas the rulers of the land do not have the ability to undertake a journey of many days from their country. For progress is slow, and he who travels on foot cannot carry provisions sufficient for a long period. By contrast, the seafarer is able to sail until he comes to friendly or weakly defended territory. This would probably have been the accepted view until the Spartan general Brasidas travelled from the Hellespont through Thrace to Amphipolis, where he defeated an Athenian force under Thucydides. It seems likely that this event post-dated X's work, taking place in 423 (?). In any case, Brasidas' feat was not to be repeated.

3. They are untroubled by crop failures caused by bad weather, "For the whole earth is not diseased at one and the same time, and so imports from an area which is flourishing reach the rulers of the sea." Ignoring the conflation of disease and bad weather as prejudicial to crops, X fails to take into account the vulnerability of the sea routes by which food is imported. Athens' grain supply came from the eastern extent of the Black Sea, a journey that passed through the Hellespont, where Persian and Spartan threats were never far away. When the Athenians were literally 'rulers of the sea,' these could be regarded with equanimity, but eventually, they forced defeat on Athens.

4. In a diversion from strategic to cultural or 'lesser' matters (2, 7-8), X confirms the cosmopolitan nature of Athens in the 420s, explaining that "through their rule of the sea they have mixed with other peoples in other

places," and so they have "discovered varieties of luxury foods... gathered together in one place." And also, "through hearing every sort of language, they have acquired for themselves this word from one language, that from another. The other Greeks stick rather to their individual language and diet and dress, whereas the Athenians employ a mixture, which comes from all the Greeks and non-Greeks." X provides no comment on whether he regards this by-product of the maritime empire as an advantage or not; however, given his wealthy background, he is likely to have benefitted more from the availability of 'luxury foods' than the typical citizen. He then wonders off the subject of sea power altogether, in a fairly neutral description of the state support for the provision of sanctuaries and sacrificial feasts that the demos are able to enjoy and which would otherwise be beyond their ability. X also remarks on the provision of exercise areas, changing rooms and baths for the *demos*, and cannot resist giving this a pejorative slant by claiming that the mob *(ochlos)* derive more enjoyment from these than the few and the well-to-do – an inversion of the way things should be.

5. X then returns to the subject of naval power, now more specifically orientated towards Athens as the exemplar. He makes the fairly comprehensive claim that the Athenians, "Alone of Greeks and non-Greeks, are able to possess naval wealth." This claim is based upon the assertion that the raw materials needed for shipbuilding, by which he means the construction of triremes – timber, iron, copper and flax – are never found together in

individual geographic locations, and so cities wishing to undertake shipbuilding must import most of the necessary raw materials. But imports by sea are, of course, subject to the scrutiny and control of the rulers of the sea, who "will prevent any of our rivals from transporting these materials as a cargo to any other place." X then abandons any pretence of a disinterested discussion with an unusually personal note: "Thus producing nothing from my land, I possess all these materials because of the sea" – and, by implication, Athens' domination of it. In the mid-420s, X, probably in common with the great majority of his fellow citizens, could not contemplate a substantive challenge to Athens' naval superiority. This self-confidence was to be maintained for another decade.

6. In a final examination of Athenian naval power, X turns from a straightforward celebration of Athenian superiority to a consideration of its disadvantages. These stem from Athens' possession of a hinterland – the province of Attica – which is vulnerable to attack by land forces, against which, as he has maintained, Athenian land forces are ineffective. This is clearly a reflection of Spartan invasions of Attica, which had been an annual occurrence from the onset of the Archidamian War. These invasions were punitive rather than overwhelming, involving the laying waste of farmland and dwellings, and necessitated the evacuation of the Attic population, or a large proportion of it, into the fortified space formed by the city and the walls connecting it to the Piraeus, which the Spartans never attempted to invest. X points out that "the farmers and the rich" suffer from these raids, and

therefore "truckle to the enemy" – which seems rather unfair and without any evidence, while the *demos*, who have no possessions outside the city (apart from their jobs it might be suggested) "since they know well that the enemy will not burn or cut down anything of theirs, live without fear, and without truckling to them." X's answer to this problem is the rather unhelpful suggestion that it would be better if Athens were located on an island where their defence would be an entirely maritime matter and thus make them invulnerable. There is an echo of Pericles' speech at the beginning of the Archidamian War, where he proposes the evacuation of the country dwellers to the city, claiming precisely that the city and its walls, providing protected access to the sea, effectively transform Athens into an island.

In the final section of his treatise, X turns to the democratic administration of the Athenian state, in particular considering two major criticisms characteristically ascribed to 'some people.' The first considers the claim that the combination of the Boule and the ekklesia operate with such tardiness that "it is sometimes not possible for the council or the assembly to do business with a person there, even though he sits waiting for a whole year." X's immediate response to this is to maintain that "This happens at Athens because of nothing other than a large amount of public business: they are not able to do business with everyone before sending them away." He then gives a lengthy recital of the deliberations to which the Boule have to undertake annually, also noting that these have to co-exist with the large number of festivals held by the city, during which no state business could be transacted. X also includes, without a separate ascription, the public work of the law courts, which complemented the decisions of the Boule, giving as examples the case "where a man does not repair his ship" and, also connected with the trierarchy, settling disputes over the annual appointment of four hundred trierarchs. Apart from these annual events, "Then, intermittently, they have to judge cases of avoidance of military service and any other sudden crime which may occur… and there are many other items which I completely pass over." X asks whether the load might be reduced but immediately responds with the impossibility of deciding which to exclude. Again, he questions the need for a large number of judges in Athenian courts and answers himself with the danger of bribery if there are only a few. After a somewhat convoluted argument, X concludes that "there is not the ability for public business at Athens to be different from the way it is now… there is no ability to make a substantial change without removing some element of the democracy itself." It might be suggested that, at this point, X comes close to defending the democracy itself rather than as a successful but deplorable socio-political construction.

Something of the same might be said of the final section in the work, which appears to be an afterthought or perhaps misplaced. In it, X considers the 'objection' raised by 'someone': "Has no one been unjustly disfranchised at Athens?" X immediately turns this into the question of whether those that have been disfranchised – i.e. lost their civic rights – who apparently number 'only a few' constitute a threat to the democracy. Typically, X answers immediately, "One needs more than a few to make an attack on the democracy at Athens." He then returns to something like the original question, although now considering the 'majority of people' – "For how could anyone think that the majority of people have been unjustly disfranchised at Athens, a state where it is the demos who hold the political offices? It is from failing to hold office justly, or to do or say what is not just, that men are disfranchised at Athens." Although answering an unspoken and pointless question, X gives what can only be described as a tribute to Athenian justice.

X's treatise displays two conflicted viewpoints. On the one hand, is his contempt for the *demos* – the *poneroi*, the worthless – inexorably locked into an endless *agon* against the *chrestoi*, the best men. On the other, he celebrates the thalassocracy that the democracy has created and maintained despite being under the control of these very same useless and immoral dregs of the society that they infest. It might be conjectured that his anti-democratic views are a product of his background and possibly the sort of companionship that a young man from a wealthy family might possess, with membership of one of the clubs – the *hetairai* – who formed a consistently anti-democratic faction, which came to the fore in the oligarchic revolts. While at the same time, perhaps under the influence of a mature and less partisan thinker, he recognises the extent to which Athens is dependent on its navy and in consequence, the lower strata of society, which mans it.

Chapter 8
The Sicilian Campaign

In 415 BC, the democratic regime in Athens launched an invasion of Sicily, involving both a large fleet and correspondingly large land forces transported by sea. In doing so, they contravened Pericles' insistence that the Athenians should restrict their operations in the war to the sea and the defence of the existing empire and avoid opening new conflicts on the land. They had recently suffered a defeat in a hoplite battle against the Spartans at Mantinea in 418. How could the Athenians undertake another theatre of operations, which would inevitably involve large-scale land actions, given this?

The answer lies in the persuasive power of one remarkable individual, Alcibiades, son of Cleinias, whose name appears continually throughout the history of the remainder of the Peloponnesian war and beyond.

Alcibiades was born into an extremely wealthy Athenian family; his father won renown for providing his own private trireme, with its crew of two hundred, during the naval engagements with the Persians. An indication of his wealth is the fact that he entered no less than seven chariot teams in the Olympic games of 418 (?) when the ability to own and maintain one horse was enough to gain recognition as a member of the second highest of the

Solonian classes, the knights or *hippeis*. Alcibiades appears in a number of Plato's dialogues, being the eponymous subject of one, also the *Theaetetus* and, notoriously, the *Symposion*, in which he shatters the rarefied intellectual atmosphere created by Socrates' disquisition on the nature of love, arriving drunk and supported by a flute girl – a common form of entertainment at Athenian drinking parties, whose contributions frequently extended beyond the musical. Plutarch compares him to a chameleon, capable of submerging himself into widely differing cultures: from the homo-eroticism of the Athenian symposium and the demotic theatre of the *ekklesia* to the grim militarism of Sparta and then the luxurious hieratic Persian court.

He first came to the attention of Thucydides after the signing of the Peace of Nicias in 421 BC. At this stage in the Archidamian war, both Athens and Sparta had reached a state of paralleled lack of success and exhaustion. Athens had failed to regain the strategically important city of Amphipolis, while Sparta was unable to dislodge the Athenians from her territory at Pylos. The respective leaders, Nicias, the Athenians' senior general and Pleistoanax, the Spartan king, were both desirous of an end to hostilities, the former because he feared that a hitherto successful career might well be threatened by further exposure to the fortunes of war, the latter because he faced continual domestic antagonism by certain factions in the Spartan state who questioned his return from a banishment of nineteen years. A peace treaty was duly signed, supposedly guaranteeing peace for fifty years and encompassing the release of the Spartan prisoners taken at Sphacteria and the restoration of Amphipolis to Athens.

Immediately, however, both sides and their allies expressed dissatisfaction with the treaty. The Athenians being particularly aggrieved at Sparta's failure to deliver Amphipolis as agreed when they had released the Spartan prisoners, and despite an envoy to Sparta undertaken by the ever more unpopular Nicias. In consequence, a war party rapidly came into existence at Athens, determined to continue hostilities, in which Alcibiades was a leading light. He had been angered by his exclusion from the negotiations leading up to the peace, to which he felt entitled to be a part as his father had been *proxenos* for Sparta at Athens, and he blamed Nicias for, as he saw it, slighting him because of his youth. He then worked assiduously to re-ignite the war with Sparta, displaying his already considerable powers to persuade a number of Peloponnesian states to ally with Athens against Sparta, resulting in the battle of Mantinea – a victory for the Spartans, as mentioned above.

Despite this setback, which appears to have left Alcibiades as confident as ever, in 416 BC, he led a force of twenty triremes to assist the democrats in Argos, who had overthrown a Sparta-friendly oligarchy and declared an alliance with Athens. Alcibiades' force took three hundred pro-Spartan oligarchs prisoner and then moved on to the island of Melos, which had been colonised by Spartans. The Athenian leaders ordered the Melians to submit to Athenian rule as a subject 'ally.' The Melians protested that they did not wish to become 'slaves' but were willing to offer friendship. The Athenians' response was a brutal display of unvarnished power politics: they did not want the Melians' friendship, to accept; it would merely signal weakness to existing members of the empire. It was either submission or destruction. The Melians courageously persisted in defying the Athenian demand and were forced to surrender their city. The Athenians put to death all males of military age and sold the women and children into slavery. It is not clear whether Alcibiades was still present on the island at this denouement; however, he must bear some of the responsibility.

In the same year, the city of Egesta in Sicily sent envoys to Athens requesting assistance in their dispute with Syracuse and Selinus, also Sicilian cities. The Athenian *ekklesia* voted to send envoys to Egesta to report on the conflict and its participants. When the envoys returned in 415, they were accompanied by Egestaeans who brought with them sixty Talents to pay for a force of sixty Athenian ships to assist them in their dispute for one month. Additionally, they gave the Athenians to understand that there was an abundance of money lying ready in the temples and the treasury of Egesta. The *ekklesia* was impressed by these indications of accessible wealth and voted to send the sixty ships to Sicily under the joint command of Alcibiades, Nicias and Lamachus, another experienced general. Their remit was to assist the Egestaeans and, should this not occupy the force entirely, to 'further in such manner as they thought best the Athenian interests in Sicily,' a distinctly open-ended instruction.

Five days later, the ekklesia met again to consider the requirements of the expedition as specified by the generals. The first (recorded) speech came from Nicias, who, according to Thucydides, had been appointed general against his will, and who recognised that those who had voted for the expedition really had in mind the conquest of Sicily, 'which was no easy task.' His speech, therefore, was intended to dissuade the assembly from going ahead with the expedition. He commenced by reminding them that they had no lack of enemies, including some of their supposed allies who had been in a state of rebellion for years. Rather than provoke the Sicilians, who posed no threat to Athens, into becoming another and powerful enemy, the right course would be to secure the Empire and leave the Egestaeans to sort out their own problems. He also delivered a withering attack on Alcibiades while, according to Thucydides, not deigning to mention him by name: "…some young man here who is delighted at holding a command, the more so because he is too young for his post… he is much admired for his stud of horses, and wants to make something of his command which will maintain him in his extravagance." Nicias went on to suggest that Alcibiades had packed the assembly with 'young men like himself' whom he suspected of intending to intimidate those against the expedition: "If any of you should be placed next to one of his supporters, I would not have him ashamed or afraid of being thought a coward if he does not vote for war." He then asked that his proposal that the expedition should be called off should be put to a vote.

Alcibiades' counterattack began with a direct response to Nicias' depiction of him as a youthful wastrel, claiming that his prodigious expenditure on chariots at the Olympic Games was to the benefit of the Athenian state in that it convinced the other Greeks that Athens was not 'exhausted by war.' He then abandoned any attempt to disguise his arrogance by refusing to accept that anyone "was on a level with him" and questioning why the recognition of his self-evident superiority should be regarded as unjust. It might be thought that this blatant egotism might have played badly with the demotic gathering to which it was exposed, yet though it was true that the people mistrusted his political motives and thought he was aiming at a tyranny, they were already dazzled by his military prowess and charisma, which outshone the dullness and reluctance of Nicias. Characteristically, he then went on to boast of his success in persuading the 'most powerful Peloponnesian states' to confront the Spartans at Mantinea, claiming that even though the Spartans were victorious, 'they have hardly recovered their courage.' Turning to the proposed Sicilian expedition, he urged the assembly to use both himself, 'in the flower of my youth,' and Nicias, 'who enjoys the reputation of success,' a somewhat tepid recommendation. He belittled the military preparedness of the Sicilians and dismissed Nicias' warnings of the enemies the expedition would be leaving behind, claiming that they were 'the same that our forefathers had' – meaning the Spartans, where Nicias had been referring to rebellious allies – and insisting that now, as then, the 'greatness of their navy' would overcome all. His peroration ended by posing the question, 'Why hesitate? ...convinced that we shall be most likely to increase our power here if we attack our enemies [meaning the unthreatening Sicilians] there, let us sail... whether we succeed and remain, or depart... the navy will ensure our safety... Nicias must not divert you from your purpose by preaching indolence and by trying to set the young against the old.' Alcibiades' speech was warmly received particularly by the Egestaeans present and also a number of Leontines, who had been thrown off their land in Sicily by the Syracusans and who had invoked the support of the Athenians, claiming a shared Ionian heritage and an old alliance.

Alcibiades' speech had the desired effect: the people were 'more than ever resolved for war.' In response, Nicias returned to the rostrum in a last attempt to prevent what he believed was a dangerous folly. Directly contradicting Alcibiades, he asserted that the Sicilians, particularly the Syracusans and Selinuntians, the enemies of the Egestaeans, were well-armed with both naval and land forces and moreover, they were self-sufficient in basic foodstuffs, as they grew their own corn – not an insignificant matter for potential targets of siege warfare. In view of this, he warned that it would be disastrous to sail with 'an insignificant force of marines': they must send a large heavy-armed force, including allies, and also, there must be sufficient food taken, with merchant ships and bakers to prepare it. As Thucydides remarks, if Nicias expected that this reality check would deter the enthusiasm of the people, he was mistaken – they were more determined than ever: "All were seized with a passionate desire to sail – the elder convinced that they would achieve the conquest of Sicily – the young longing to see the marvels of a distant land – the troops expected to receive present pay and to conquer a country that would be an inexhaustible supply of pay for the future." Already, the limited aims of the expedition had been overtaken by the ambition of the complete conquest of the island.

Eventually, the crowd's impatience was crystallised by an intervention by one of its members who demanded that Nicias abandon his Cassandran prophecies and simply state what forces would be necessary to achieve success. With considerable reluctance, probably realising that the assembly was prepared to vote for anything, Nicias specified at least one hundred triremes, some of which would be troop carriers, to transport five thousand hoplites and a proportionate number of archers and Cretan slingers. Without delay, the assembly decreed that the generals should be empowered to act as they thought best in terms of both numbers and management of the expedition.

The preparations for the expedition were interrupted by a strange event, the "Mutilation of the herms." The herms were quadrangular carved stone pillars, each surmounted by a head and with an erect phallus on the front, and were symbolic of the god Hermes, particularly his powers of fertility and ability both to ward off bad luck and provide its opposite. Herms were very popular in Athens, found very frequently in front of house entrances, and during a single night, a large number of them were vandalised by having their heads mutilated. The effect on the Athenians was, perhaps surprisingly, very considerable: they immediately suspected that this was intended to foment civil disturbance, leading to an attempt to overthrow the democracy, suggesting that the Old Oligarch's confidence in the robustness of the regime was less than well justified. This civic alarm was further exacerbated by a rumour that wealthy young men had been profaning the Eleusian mysteries by celebrating them, presumably in a disrespectful way, in private houses. (The nature of the Eleusian mysteries, which were publicly celebrated in one of the few specifically religious ceremonies, remains a mystery itself to this day.) Despite the political advancement of the Athenians, they were notably conservative in religious matters and profanity and blasphemy were taken extremely seriously, and these events were thought to augur badly for the forthcoming expedition. The preparations were further complicated by information laid by 'certain metics and slaves' – categories who would not normally be given much credence – which implicated Alcibiades in the impiety supposedly inflicted on the mysteries. This was seized upon eagerly by a faction who were jealous of Alcibiades' influence over the people, who maliciously extended the charges against him to include the mutilation of the herms and a confirmation of a conspiracy against the democracy. Alcibiades strongly denied the charges and offered to stand trial before he sailed – the expeditionary force now being ready. His accusers were against this, fearing that the assembled military might well support him, and demanded, via planted speakers in the assembly, that the expedition should not be delayed and that Alcibiades should sail with it and be recalled when the case against him had been properly established. Their intention was to reinforce the feeling against him, a task that would be made easier without his charismatic presence. The assembly agreed that he should sail.

The departure of the expeditionary fleet was attended with great ceremony and an explosion of civic pride at the realisation of the military might that had been assembled. This laid to rest some of the forebodings that had begun to afflict the populace as a result of both a growing appreciation of the possible risks involved and also the unfortunate resonances of the rumoured anti-democratic conspiracy. These were submerged, at least temporarily, in the wave of confidence that swept virtually the entire population of Athens down to the Piraeus, where the fleet and the soldiers were assembled. The fleet consisted of one hundred triremes, of which sixty were 'swift-sailing' – warships of the line – and forty transports for carrying the five thousand hoplites. The ships were provided as empty hulls, which were then fitted out by their trierarchs. The enthusiasm with which the trierarchs undertook their liturgy can be gauged by Thucydides' remark that 'everyone strove to the utmost that his own ship might excel both in beauty and swiftness… the figure-heads and other fittings were of the most costly description.' They were also responsible for the manning of their ships, 'with the best crews that could be obtained.' This raises the interesting question as to how knowledge of 'the best crews' was available when there is no historical evidence supporting the contemporary existence of 'lists' of trireme crews, unlike the case for hoplites where 'The infantry had been well-selected and the lists carefully made up.' However they were chosen, the trierarchs are reported as having supplemented the state pay for rowers, for the upper rank only – the *thranitai,* and also the petty officers, who generally appear to have been Athenian citizens – from their own pockets.

When the men and equipment had been embarked, the hubbub was silenced by a trumpet blast. A herald then led the fleet, and the watching citizens, in the recital of the 'customary prayers,' then the deck crews – the *hyperesia* and the marines, together presumably with the trierarchs – 'mingling wine in bowls' made libations from vessels of gold and silver. An interesting feature of the recruitment of the fleet personnel is that seven hundred of the 'infantry' were *thetes* who had signed up as marines, roles usually, supposedly, occupied by the hoplite class, the *zeugitai*. This is probably an indication of the obsolescence of the Solonian classes by this point in the fifth century and also perhaps of the democratising effect of shipboard life, where the cramped conditions led to citizens possessed of colossal wealth being literally cheek by jowl with those from the lowest classes and non-citizens. Whatever the reason, it seems very likely that some of the pourers and consumers of the wine from the elegant receptacles were *thetes* rubbing shoulders with the trierarchs.

Following the completion of the libations, the crews raised the paean (war cry), and the ships set sail, leaving in line astern and then, in keeping with the regatta-like atmosphere, they raced each other to the island of Aegina. From there, they sailed to Corcyra on the northwest coast of Greece, where the allies who formed the rest of the expeditionary force were assembling, amounting to an additional thirty-four triremes, mainly from Chios. As well as warships and transports, there were thirty merchant ships with provisions and bakers, masons, carpenters and tools for siege warfare.

This combined fleet then sailed to the Italian coast and divided into three squadrons, each allocated to one of the three generals. Each squadron had sent one ship ahead in a preliminary foray to ascertain where the fleet would be welcome and forewarn the main body. The reports were not generally favourable. Many of the Greek settlements on the coast refused to allow the personnel of the fleet within their walls or even, in some cases, to allow them water and anchorage. When they reached Rhegium, on the extreme south-easterly point of Italy, they were again refused entry to the city despite its having been a recognised ally of Athens, but the inhabitants provided a market for them and permitted the ships to be drawn up ashore, and the crews rested in an encampment. The preceding trio of ships then returned from Egesta, where they had gone on to determine whether the money that the Egestaeans had promised was available. Their report was a disappointment – only thirty Talents were forthcoming, and nothing more – falling far short of what the Alcibiades and Lamachos had expected, although Nicias was not surprised, in line with his doubts over the whole enterprise.

The generals then held a council of war. Nicias took the opportunity provided by the disappointment felt by the other two to argue for a limited plan of action, restricting it to threatening the Selinuntians with the entire fleet and bringing them to come to terms with the Egestaeans – the original motivation for the expedition. They would then display Athenian might by sailing along the Sicilian coast and return home. Alcibiades urged that it would be a disgrace to have set off with such a force and return with nothing. He suggested that they should pursue a policy of winning over the Sicilian cities, other than Selinus and Syracuse, so that they would join them in attacking the latter, an idea doubtless inspired by his faith in his powers of persuasion. But first, he proposed that they should appeal to the Messenians, whose harbour commanded the sea route to Sicily and would provide the ideal base for the Athenians to watch the enemy. Alcibiades blandishments, however, proved unequal to the task of persuading the Messenians to allow the fleet to use their port, although he appears to have sowed the seeds of a conspiracy amongst the pro-Athenian faction in the city to betray it to the fleet at a later date. Lamachos suggested an immediate direct assault on Syracuse, relying on surprise and the notion that 'new enemies are always more terrible at first,' an idea not without its validity. Thucydides maintains that Lamachos then backed Alcibiades' plan, but the resulting action seems to have owed more to him. In the event, they sailed to Syracuse, sending ten ships into the Great Harbour on a reconnaissance to determine whether a Syracusan fleet had been launched. On ascertaining that this was not the case, they had a herald proclaim that the Athenians had come to restore their allies and kinsmen, the Leontines, to their homes and inviting any in Syracuse to join them. They then surveyed the area of potential conflict and, with the remainder of the fleet, sailed away, leaving the Syracusans no doubt relieved but also less than overawed.

The campaign then continued in a somewhat desultory fashion with an abortive excursion to the city of Camarina, having been told that they would be welcome there – which proved to be false. On the return journey, they landed on Syracusan territory and laid to waste a small area, losing a number of light-armed soldiers to enemy cavalry in the process. On returning to their base, now at Catana, they beheld an unwelcome sight: the 'sacred ship' *Salaminia*, which was fully owned and manned by the Athenian state and used for state business, and which had been sent to bring back Alcibiades to stand trial in Athens for 'profaning the mysteries and the mutilation of the herms.'

In his absence, the Athenians had prosecuted their enquiries into these two outrages as keenly as ever, their efforts, however, degenerating into a witch hunt, with little attempt to verify the flood of dubious testimony which frequently implicated innocent citizens. Alcibiades' enemies had succeeded in focusing the Athenian citizenry's generalised disquiet against him, particularly on the charge of profaning the mysteries and also the associated rumour of an anti-democratic, pro-Spartan conspiracy. This had been co-incidentally reinforced by the appearance of a Spartan raiding party in the Corinthian isthmus, which had not approached Athens but induced a state of panic, leading to a popular demand for Alcibiades to be tried and executed. The *Salaminia* was accordingly dispatched.

The officials on board the *Salaminia* did not arrest Alcibiades in order not to disturb the expeditionary force or to attract the attention of the enemy but instructed him to follow them in his own ship. On reaching Thurii on the Italian coast, they stopped for the night – a standard procedure for trireme voyages – during which he slipped away from his ship with a number of others also wanted for trial and disappeared. The crew of the *Salaminia* tried to find him without success and returned to Athens, where he was condemned to death in his absence. Shortly after, Alcibiades crossed over from Thurii to Peloponnesus in a small boat.

During the winter that followed, the Athenians prepared for an attack on Syracuse, and the Syracusans prepared to repel it. The Syracusans were emboldened by another Athenian failure – an attack on the city of Hybla, which was repulsed – leading to a demand that their generals should attack the Athenian camp at Catana. Hearing of this, the Athenians developed a plan for the attack on Syracuse, which played to the populace's bellicosity. They found a Catanian who was known to the Syracusans but was well disposed towards the Athenians. He was dispatched to Syracuse to convince their generals that the Athenians were in the habit of abandoning their camp overnight, leaving their weapons, preferring to take their ease in the city. An attack on the camp by a strong force from Syracuse early in the morning would literally catch the Athenians napping and weaponless and be overwhelmed as they tried to regroup. As a final inducement, the story included a promise that the Catanians would fire the Athenian ships in the harbour. The aim of the plan was to ensure an undefended city when the Athenian forces arrived by ship at Syracuse.

In their confident mood, the Syracusans swallowed this story and, on the eve of the appointed day, set out with their entire force towards Catana, more or less simultaneously with the Athenians embarking their force prior to an overnight sail to Syracuse, where they landed their troops unopposed, and took up position at a previously identified spot. It might have been thought that, given the apparent success of the plan, and the resulting lack of opposition, the Athenians would have attempted to invest the city immediately; however, consistent with Nicias' risk-averse tactics, they applied themselves to improving the defences of an already easily defended position, outside the city walls. The Syracusan cavalry, having ridden ahead of the main force, were the first to discover that the Athenians had gone with their fleet and turned back to apprise their comrades and lead a hasty retreat back to Syracuse. When they arrived, they discovered the Athenians in a well-fortified position, deliberately chosen to be difficult for a cavalry attack in recognition of their deficiency in cavalry numbers. They made no attempt to confront the Syracusan force, and so the day ended with a stand-off under the city walls.

On the morrow, Nicias lost no time in leading his force against the Syracusans, some of whom had gone for the night into the city and who were somewhat unready for the fight. Although they recovered rapidly and fought well, they were gradually forced back and eventually broke and fled. The Athenians, however, were unable to follow up their advantage by pursuing the fleeing Syracusans because their numerous cavalry attacked the Athenian hoplites as they, necessarily, broke their ranks. Eventually, the Athenians, despite their 'victory,' ended up being penned in the defensive position to which they had returned, and the Syracusan army was allowed to escape to the city. As winter was at hand, and with their lack of cavalry, Nicias decided that they could do no more in Sicily until they had more horsemen from both Athens and their Sicilian allies and more money from both these sources, and they sailed away.

The Athenians had expected to over-winter in Messene, where a group of plotters encouraged by Alcibiades on his apparently fruitless visit there had agreed to betray the city and port to them. However, on being relieved of his command and having absconded, Alcibiades had contacted a pro-Syracuse faction in the city and revealed the plot to them, and they immediately exterminated the plotters. The Athenians were turned away and went on to Naxos for the winter, where they sent a request to Athens for reinforcements, particularly of horsemen and money.

This was not the only disservice that Alcibiades performed for his ex-comrades, and the next was considerably more damaging. His escape to Peloponnesus had not gone unnoticed by the Spartans, and they invited him to Sparta. Having received safe conduct, he travelled there and was further invited to address the Spartan assembly. By a remarkable coincidence, he appeared at the same time as envoys from Syracuse and Corinth, who had come to urge the Spartans to open hostilities against Athens so as to divert the Athenians from their plans to invade Syracuse. The ephors (Spartan magistrates) were minded to go as far as encouraging the Syracusans to resist the Athenians but had been reluctant to commit to anything further. Then Alcibiades addressed the assembly.

He began by reminding the Spartans of his family's historical friendship with them as *proxenoi* and claimed to have performed many 'good offices' for them after their 'misfortune' at Pylos. He then played down his family's commitment to the democratic regime at Athens, knowing full well his audiences' antipathy to democracy, maintaining that 'we did our best to observe political moderation amid the prevailing licence.' Then, in a remarkable piece of hypocrisy for one who had swayed the assembly behind his plan for the Sicilian expedition, he lamented the existence of demagogues 'who led the people into evil ways.' Moving onto the expedition itself, he described its objectives in terms which would have surprised its most enthusiastic supporters, of domination of the whole of Greece.

He claimed that the Syracusans would not be able to hold out against the Athenians, and once Syracuse submitted, the whole of Sicily would be in their hands. In turn, the Athenians would overrun the Greek colonies in Italy, using its abundance of timber to build many more triremes with which to blockade and then invade Peloponnesus. He insisted that Sparta should send a force of hoplites to Sicily, who would 'handle the oars' of their ships and, particularly, a Spartan commander who would organise resistance to the Athenians. He also, according to Thucydides, suggested that the Spartans should occupy and fortify the outpost at Decelea, which was only a short distance from Athens. With a remarkable gift of foresight, or Thucydides' hindsight, he predicted that the Athenians' slaves would desert en mass to them, and they would cut Athens off from the revenue they obtained from the silver mines at Laurium. (It may not have passed Alcibiades' notice that Nicias derived his not inconsiderable wealth from the ownership of one thousand slaves working in these same silver mines.) Alcibiades terminated his peroration by asking the Spartans not to think worse of him as a traitor to his country, claiming that he had lost 'an ungrateful country... which I am seeking to regain' and assuring them that his knowledge of Athens' secrets would be invaluable to them.

The Spartans were impressed by this speech, which strengthened their existing intention to send an army against Athens. Accordingly, they took up Alcibiades' suggestion of the fortification of Decelea and also to send a Spartan commander to lead the Syracusan forces, choosing Gylippus for the role. He was to be provided with a small number of ships by the Corinthians.

At the end of the winter in 414, the Athenians received the request for additional cavalry and money, and the assembly, apparently without demur, voted 300 Talents of silver and 250 horsemen, with their equipment but no horses: they were expected to purchase them in Sicily. In addition, when these reinforcements arrived and sailed to Syracuse with the rest of the Athenian forces, they were joined by 300 Egestaean horsemen and 100 others. With these strengthened numbers, they prevented the Syracusans from occupying Epipolae, a piece of highland overlooking the city into which they drove back their forces. They then began to build a wall around the city, a standard technique in contemporary Greek siege warfare. Nothing daunted, the Syracusans then began to build their own wall radially from the city and intended to intersect the Athenian's circumvallation. These walls and their constructors became the focus for many more or less serious skirmishes between the opposing forces. During one of these, the Athenian general Lamachos was killed, leaving Nicias, who was suffering from a chronic kidney disease, in sole charge. Although progress was slow, eventually, the Athenian's wall was nearly complete.

At this point, the position of the Syracusans appeared to offer little hope; they had been expecting help from the Peloponnesians, particularly the Spartans, but none had arrived. However, after a fraught journey, during which his handful of ships had been swept off course and damaged, and he had been wrongly advised that the Athenians had completed their wall and had given up Sicily for lost, Gylippus, with his ships refitted and receiving intelligence that Syracuse had not been invested, finally arrived in Sicily and set about recruiting allies including the Selinuntians and others friendly to Syracuse. Nicias had been aware of Gylippus' approach but had contemptuously dismissed him as a threat, presumably because of the apparently small size of his forces. Gylippus' arrival coincided with that of a Corinthian naval force, the commander of which spoke to the Syracusan assembly, which was on the point of suing for peace, and apprised them of Gylippus's arrival and persuaded them to continue their resistance to the Athenians. Gylippus then arrived at Syracuse with about three thousand men and immediately attempted to seize the heights continue of Epipolae but was dissuaded from engaging with the Athenians there as his forces were unprepared for a major confrontation. Shortly after, Nicias recognising that the Syracusan counter-wall, the construction of which was being assisted by Gylippus' force, was nearing the point where it would neutralise the Athenians' circumvallation, decided that he must attack to prevent this. He was presented with an opportunity when Gylippus stationed his forces beneath the city wall and in a position hemmed in by the newly built wall. He attacked with his heavy-armed troops, and the Syracusan defenders, being unable to deploy their cavalry because of the restricted space, were defeated and forced back into the city. Gylippus admitted that his tactics had led to the defeat and ensured that they would not be repeated in the next confrontation with the Athenians when he took the initiative and stationed his forces away from the walls, thus allowing both his cavalry and light-armed troops –

javelin men and slingers – to manoeuvre around and outflank the enemy's hoplites. (It may be wondered what had happened to the cavalry reinforcements that the Athenians had received. Thucydides is silent on the question.) The result was a defeat for Nicias and, effectively, the end of any hopes that he had for taking Syracuse by land.

Recognising that his situation was steadily worsening, Nicias sent a letter to the Athenian assembly describing it in some detail:

The arrival of Gylippus with his 'army' (not mentioning the fact that it consisted of a motley collection of Syracuse's allies and recently armed sailors from his ships) had entirely altered the position of the Athenian force. They had been forced back to their defensive position, and now they were the besieged rather than the besiegers. Moreover, Gylippus, Nicias was informed, was actively seeking reinforcements from Peloponnesus, which might well take the form of Spartan troops.

The Athenian fleet was deteriorating rapidly, both in the physical condition of the ships, which were waterlogged as the result of their crews' inability to beach them to dry them out due to enemy control of the litoral, and also the morale and discipline of the crews whose numbers were also dwindling through desertion and casualties suffered when they foraged for food. (He gives some interesting insights into the declining efficiency of trireme rowers during an extended period of service Thuc VII, 11). At the same time, the Syracusans had been developing their own naval force and would soon be in a position to blockade the Athenians' supporters in Italy, who were supplying them with provisions.

In conclusion, their current situation was untenable. The assembly must decide either that it wished the expedition to continue its mission, in which case it must send another force of equivalent size to the one that was originally sent, or it must recall them. Nicias also apprised them of his illness and requested a replacement to take command.

Despite the barely relieved pessimism of Nicias' letter, the assembly maintained its ill-founded faith in the superiority of their forces, particularly the navy, and voted to send another sixty ships with 1200 heavy-armed troops under the generals Eurymedon and Demosthenes, the victor of Pylos. Nicias was not released from his command, but two of his colleagues in Sicily were advanced to equal him in rank to share the burden.

At more or less the same time, the Syracusans were successful in persuading the Corinthians and Lacedaemonians to send forces in their support, including hoplites who were transported to the island by merchant ship. Alcibiades' campaign to persuade the Lacedaemonians to establish a base at Decelea, only fourteen miles from Athens, now bore fruit as they despatched a force under the Spartan King Agis to fortify and occupy the existing stronghold. Their presence rapidly reduced the Athenians to, in Thucydides' words, desperation. Twenty thousand slaves deserted the city to seek the protection of the Spartans (considering the contrasting ways in which slaves were treated in Athens and Sparta, this seems surprising), and, as Alcibiades had predicted, the Athenians were cut off from the silver mines at Laurium, and their financial position had become had precarious, and their need for cash so immediate that they abandoned the collection of tribute from their imperial subjects, instead imposing a five per cent harbour tax on all imports and exports.

Before Demosthenes arrived with the reinforcements, Gylippus undertook an attack by land and sea on three Athenian forts that they had constructed on a spit of land that almost closed the Grand Harbour at Syracuse. The Athenians were victorious in the sea battle, but their forts were overcome on the land. This was a very considerable loss, not only for the men and material involved, which included the gear for forty triremes, but it also left the Athenians unable to land provisions arriving by sea.

During this period, the Athenians, whose resources were not entirely absorbed by the Sicilian expedition, fought a sea battle with the Corinthians in the Gulf of Corinth off Naupactus, where the inhabitants were largely freed helots, and their descendants, who had been domiciled there under the protection of the Athenians after the helot revolt and were friendly to them. The battle was 'long and obstinate' according to Thucydides but ended inconclusively. However, it was significant for a technological development on the part of the Corinthians, who were perhaps the first mainland Greeks to use the trireme. Their innovation, which in some ways might seem to have been a retrograde step, was to shorten and reinforce the bows of their ships, thus enabling them to withstand a prow-to-prow collision with a conventional trireme without damage, while the conventional ship's bow would be stove in, rendering the ship unserviceable. Conventional trireme tactics relied on ramming an enemy ship at its weakest point, amidships, and at high speed to avoid damage to the attacking ship. This was a more lethal attack than that resulting from the prow-to-prow model of the Corinthians, often resulting in the splitting of the attacked vessel into two, the bow section with its heavy bronze beak tending to sink, and with consequent heavy casualties amongst the crew. This form of attack, perfected by the Athenians, also required considerable skill on the part of the steersman and rowers to perform the necessary manoeuvre, often following a path around the stern of the enemy ship and then overtaking it to a point where the midship could be rammed by a turn towards it. Also, and significantly, ships undertaking this type of manoeuvre required a considerable amount of sea-space. In the battle off Naupactus, the Athenians sank three Corinthian ships using their standard tactics, but had seven of their own damaged and made useless with their bows stove in by head-on attack. News of this reached Sicily as the Corinthians sailed there to support the Syracusans, who lost no time in modifying their own ships in this manner, recognising not only that this form of fighting would place fewer demands on their relatively inexperienced crews but also that this would place them at an advantage in the naval actions that they would be fighting in the constricted space of the Grand Harbour, where normal trireme tactics would be impossible. These expectations turned out to be justified in the next sea battle, which inevitably took place in the Grand Harbour, where the Athenians were effectively imprisoned and where the Syracusans damaged many Athenian ships by prow-to-prow attacks and sank seven, giving them the victory.

Shortly afterward, Demosthenes and Eurymedon arrived with some seventy-three ships, five thousand heavy-armed troops, and many javelin men and slingers. The Syracusans, fresh from their recent sea victory and convinced of their superiority on both land and sea, were taken aback by this demonstration of Athens' depth of resources, and reputedly, a faction in the city contacted Nicias to explore the possibility of surrender. Gylippus, however, continued with his efforts to augment the Syracusan forces.

Demosthenes was determined not to follow Nicias' delay in attacking, thus incurring the enemy's contempt, and decided on an immediate full-scale assault on the Syracusan forces on the heights of Epipolae, where they had erected a fort. He recognised that a daylight attack on a well-defended position would be, to say the least, hazardous and, with typical Athenian boldness, opted for a night-time attack. Initially, this was successful; the Athenians captured the Syracusan fort, but a number of the garrison escaped and were able to warn Gylippus, who quickly assembled his forces to meet the oncoming Athenians. The latter continued to make headway against the retreating Syracusans, but as the pursuit continued in the dark, they became disorganised and fragmented and increasingly vulnerable to the regrouping Syracusans, now reinforced by the force from the city. Eventually, the Athenians were reduced to a leaderless rabble, desperately seeking to escape in small groups or individuals. Many of those who were part of the original expedition and were familiar with the lie of the land were able to reach the Athenian encampment, but the recent reinforcements frequently became lost and were cut down in large numbers by the defenders. Finally, the Athenians were forced to ask for a truce to retrieve their dead, and the Syracusan celebrated yet another victory.

In the subsequent council of war, the Athenian generals took stock of their situation, which was unremittingly gloomy. They had been defeated both on land and sea – where they were supposedly masters. Their soldiers were demoralised and moreover were 'distressed by sicknesses, ascribed to unhealthy conditions in their camp, which was on marshy ground. (It has been suggested that this pestilence was malaria, which had been becoming more prevalent towards the end of the fifth century.) Demosthenes spoke against remaining. The 'shock and awe' attack on Epipolae had failed, and there was now little hope of defeating the Syracusans in a war of attrition with their increasing support from Sparta, the Corinthians and the rest of Sicily, while their own troops and ships were steadily deteriorating. At the same time, the city of Athens was under imminent threat from the Spartan force at Decelea, and what remained of their forces should be returned to protect against them. Nicias was characteristically undecided but maintained a public commitment to staying, saying that they would be censured by the Athenian assembly and probably be accused of treason by their soldiers. It would be better to die honourably than to return to disgrace. He also maintained that he was in contact with elements of the Syracusan populace who wished to surrender and was convinced that they should continue the siege. Unable to agree, the Athenians stayed where they were.

This indecision was brought to an end by the news that Gylippus had gathered a large body of reinforcements from Peloponnesus. Now, even Nicias was persuaded that departure was necessary, and orders were given to the men to prepare for an exodus. They were about to sail at night when an eclipse of the full moon occurred, arousing the superstitions of the men (Nicias included) who demanded that departure should be delayed. The necessary period was determined to be thrice nine days by the seers, and so the Athenians remained.

Hearing of the Athenians' thwarted departure, the Syracusans were more emboldened than ever and determined on another attack. In this third sea battle, seventy-six Syracusan ships defeated eighty-six Athenians, destroying their entire right wing and killing General Eurymedon, who commanded it together with the crews. In addition, the Athenians lost a further eighteen ships as they were trapped in the inner harbour.

The Syracusans, sensing that final victory was within their grasp, devised the intention to capture the entire Athenian fleet by entrapping it within the Grand Harbour, where it was currently moored. They began to seal the Harbour by assembling a motley collection of ships moored broadside across the harbour mouth. The Athenians, seeing the Syracusan activity, realised that they were becoming trapped and held a council of war. They decided to man their entire remaining fleet, amounting to some one hundred and ten ships, in varying states of seaworthiness, and to attempt a breakout.

Following their recent sea-borne defeat, morale in the fleet was low, and Nicias attempted to raise the men's spirits by exhortation. He reminded them of the Athenians' great experience of naval warfare and victory and how the fortunes of war could permit 'sudden reversals' permitting them to retrieve their defeat. He warned them that, because of the restricted space in the harbour, they would be obliged to fight 'a land battle on ship-board,' and so they would be embarking many more deck forces than usual, with archers and javelin men in addition to a greater than the normal complement of marines — i.e., heavy-armed hoplites. He went on to assert that 'there are no more ships like these in the Piraeus, and that you have no more young men fit for service,' so that defeat would lead immediately by the invasion of Athens by the Spartans. (Nicias includes in his speech a special message to 'some of you have long been deemed Athenians, although they are not.' This has been interpreted by some scholars as indicating that the crews were generally metics, but Thucydides makes it clear that the reference was to non-subject allies of Athens.)

In his corresponding, and probably imagined, speech, Gylippus, in addition to the conventional exhortatory passages, suggests that the Athenians' attempt to prepare for the 'land battle on ship-board' by reinforcing their deck-crews might redound against them, simply causing confusion amongst those unused to fighting on ship-board and possibly unbalancing their ships.

When the Athenians finally began to row for the harbour mouth, the Syracusans were already deployed around the harbour, as well as at the barrier of ships, and so the ensuing battle almost immediately became a disorganised melee involving some two hundred ships. Nicias' prediction was correct in so far as the futility of attempting the standard manoeuvres of sea-fighting was concerned, but there was none of the discipline of phalanx warfare that usually applied to land battles. So great was the press of ships that, individually, they had little chance of a straightforward line of attack against an enemy but invariably fouled one another or were struck even as they struck a target. The noise of the crashing vessels, together with the cheering of the deck crews, made it impossible for the rowers to hear the instructions of their boatswains, and so they lost their synchronisation and way. Eventually, the Athenians were put to flight, and those sufficiently seaworthy were driven back to the land near their encampment, where their land forces were waiting. Some of these attempted to defend the ships, while others prepared for an assault on their fortifications, but the greater number looked to their own safety and fled.

Early on the next day, Demosthenes, having ascertained the number of ships still operational to be slightly greater than those of the Syracusan force, persuaded Nicias that a further attempt should be made to break out of the harbour. Nicias agreed to this; however, the crews, when ordered, refused to board their ships, being so demoralised by this latest and most disastrous defeat. This shameful episode illustrates the extent of the catastrophe – the Athenian navy, which represented the power of the *demos* and had established a reputation of invincibility arising from the great victory of Salamis and augmented by countless actions over the subsequent decades, reduced to abandoning, and burning, its ships.

This is not the place to recount the details of the desperate and unsuccessful attempt by Nicias and Demosthenes to save their defeated force. They attempted to reach the supposedly friendly territory of the Sicels, but they were harried constantly by the Syracusan and Lacedaemonian forces and were eventually forced to capitulate, with their numbers drastically reduced by enemy action and sickness. Nicias and Demosthenes were both executed immediately, and the rest imprisoned in a quarry in appalling conditions, which increased the death toll considerably more. Eventually, most of the survivors were sold as slaves, and a handful escaped and managed to return to Athens to convey the terrible story to an unbelieving populace.

Chapter 9
Sicily – The Aftermath and the Re-emergence of Persia

The news of the disaster that had overtaken the Sicilian expedition was met initially with disbelief by the Athenian *demos:* how could the armada that had set out with such high-spirited confidence and such colossal expenditure on ships and men have been so utterly vanquished? And inevitably, as the terrible truth was confirmed by the tiny handful of survivors who arrived back at Athens, often escapees from the slavery into which they had been sold, this disbelief was transformed into anger against the orators, amongst them Alcibiades and the 'soothsayers and prophets' who had assured them that the conquest of Sicily would be easily achieved. The anger was probably amplified by the unspoken recollection of the eagerness with which the assembly had been persuaded by these false prophets.

With the disbelief and anger came also fear. The loss of a 'host of cavalry and hoplites and the flower of their youth,' the few ships remaining in the docks and the lack of crews to man even them all were easily visible to the citizenry as indicative of the weakness of the state. Less immediately visible but significant all the same was the loss of wealth to the city of the one hundred or so of its richest men who had gone as *trierarchs* with the expedition. This was on top of the loss of income from the silver mines resulting from the Spartan occupation of Decelea, which was still in force and growing ever more threatening. This was only one of the threats: as Thucydides remarks, 'Everywhere they looked, there was trouble.'

Astonishingly, despite the severity of the shock that Athens had received and the magnitude of the dangers threatening from all sides, the democratic administration managed to muster a positive response with the immediate objective of building a new navy, maintaining its faith in sea power despite the recent failure. In order to support this and provide the necessary money for the purchase of timber and the construction of the ships, they adopted a policy of economising expenditure, appointing a council of older men to advise on appropriate measures. In an unusually revealing aside, Thucydides sneeringly remarks, 'In the manner of a democracy they were very amenable to discipline while their fright lasted,' a somewhat gratuitous comment on what might be regarded as a commendable display of resilience, particularly when contrasted with his description of the fragility of oligarchy in the face of a comparatively minor setback, as will be seen.

The full catalogue of impending threats was indeed intimidating. Apart from the Spartan force at Decelea, now of considerable size and led by the able King Agis, there was every expectation that the Sicilian forces led by Syracuse but with Peloponnesian allies, including Corinth and the Boeotians would attack from the sea and many of the Athenians' 'subject states' and their supposed allies such as Chios and Lesbos were eager to take the opportunity of breaking free from Athens and possibly to join in the destruction of what appeared to be a moribund state. And now, to cap it all, after half a century of quiescence, Persia reappeared, not as a threat to Greece as a whole, but specifically to Athens and allied to the Spartans.

The reassertion of Persian enmity was the result of the desire of the new 'Great King' Darius to re-establish the tribute payments from the coastal provinces and islands of the eastern Aegean, which had been interrupted by Athens' imperial control. Two of Darius' governors, Tissaphernes in the coastal region and Pharnabazus in the Hellespont were vying with each other to bring about the eradication of Athenian power by a policy of persuading Athenian subject allies and allies to revolt, with both seeking Spartan naval assistance. Tissaphernes had sent an envoy with an embassy sent by the oligarchic faction in Chios, supposedly one of Athens' most important allies, to Sparta to seek assistance in breaking free from Athens, while Pharnabazus was attempting to persuade the Spartans to send a fleet to the Hellespont. This resulted in a 'vehement' competition between the two for the ear of the Spartan authorities. The joint Chian/Persian approach was supported in Sparta by none other than Alcibiades, who had a family connection with one of the ephors, the powerful magistrates who shared power with the dual kings.

Alcibiades, as usual, was convinced that his legendary powers of persuasion would enable him to spread revolt throughout Athens' subject states in the east Aegean and Asian coast and persuaded the ephors to authorise the sending of a fleet, which Agis had been assembling, to Chios to assist in their liberation from Athens. The fleet would be led by Chalcideus, a Spartan, accompanied by Alcibiades. After a number of vicissitudes, including being trapped in a remote harbour by an Athenian force, which took them by surprise as they were convinced that none such existed, they reached Chios, 'to the great wonder and alarm of the people,' and persuaded the council, which the oligarchs had arranged to be in session, to revolt from Athens – another triumph for Alcibiades' oratory.

When the Athenians heard of the disaffection of the Chians, they were taken aback at the prospect of the loss of their major ally. The level of their alarm is shown by the fact that they abrogated the law that provided for the death penalty for anyone even suggesting that the One Thousand Talent emergency fund, which had remained untouched for fourteen years, might be made available for the use of the state and indeed it was so used for the accelerated production of more warships for the navy. The assembly also voted to send as large a force as could be assembled to attempt to dissuade the Chians from seceding from the alliance.

The following months present a confusing picture as the Spartan-led Peloponnesian fleet and various smaller Athenian fleets manoeuvred around the eastern Aegean, attempting either to persuade subject allies of the Athenians to revolt, or to dissuade them from doing so, with varying degrees of success, occasionally being forced into fighting engagements, of limited commitment of forces, with both sides displaying a reluctance to involve their full strength: the Athenians because of an understandable fear of sustaining heavy losses, which would threaten Athens' very existence, the Peloponnesians because of the characteristic lack of confidence in naval warfare of the Spartan leadership, despite their considerable numerical superiority. During this period, however, a number of events with mid to long-term significance did occur.

The Spartan commander Chalcideus signed a treaty with Tissaphernes, on behalf, respectively, of the Spartan nation and the Great King, which essentially recognised the king's dominion over all his and his forefathers' previous possessions in Ionia (modern Turkey essentially) and the Aegean islands, together with the tribute payments which the Athenian control over these possessions had interrupted. The two powers agreed to make war on Athens until both agreed to stop. Shortly after this treaty was signed, Chalcideus was killed in a minor skirmish, and his place was taken by another Spartan admiral, Astyochus.

The island state of Samos as yet remained loyal to its alliance with Athens, and its harbour was in regular use by Athenian naval forces, three of whose ships were moored there when the Samian *demos* rebelled against the oligarchic rulers of the state. The crews of the Athenian ships took part in this uprising, confirming that the traditional democratic spirit prevailed still in the navy, at least in its lower ranks. The Athenian *demos,* assured of the fidelity of the democratic government that was then installed, granted the Samians independence. Thenceforth, Samos became a very important Athenian naval base, one which was to play a major role (in fact, two) in the next violent perturbation that was to afflict Athenian democracy.

The island of Chios was subjected to a blockade and raiding by the Athenians, which reduced their confidence in their supposed new allies, the Spartans, whose promised naval support had failed to materialise. The Spartan governor, Pedaritus, installed over the Chians, demanded that Astyochus send the fleet to relieve the island, but this was rejected. Pedaritus expressed his dissatisfaction with Astyochus in a direct message to Sparta. The result was, characteristically, the sending of a commission of eleven Spartan 'advisors' to assist Astyochus and also to keep an eye on him and possibly deprive him of his command rather than the military force that had been expected. The commission looked into, amongst many other matters, the treaty that had been signed by Chalcideus. The matter was discussed with Tissaphernes, the Persian signatory, and the Spartan Lachas expressed strong disapproval of the treaty as written, maintaining that it envisaged the enslavement of the Hellenic populations of Iona and the islands and that The Spartans, who had entered the Peloponnesian war ostensibly to 'free the Hellenes' from Athenian imperialism were loath to see this simply replaced by Persian hegemony. Tissaphernes left the meeting 'in a rage,' and the embryonic Spartan/Persian alliance received its first setback.

At much the same time, Sparta's patience with Alcibiades was wearing thin as he continued to press for positive military action on the leadership of the expedition. Eventually, the Spartan government, under the influence of King Agis, who hated Alcibiades for the not-insignificant reason that he had seduced his wife and fathered a child on her, sent a message to the expedition to kill him. Alcibiades, as usual, learnt of this before the intended recipients of the message and rapidly decamped to join Tissaphernes, who took him on as an advisor, no doubt, in order to irritate the Spartans. Alcibiades, now under threat of execution from both the Spartans and the Athenians, was placed in a position to wish a plague on both their houses, which he did by advising Tissaphernes to strengthen the king's position by weakening both of the Hellenic powers. He suggested that he should continue the appearance of support for the Peloponnesian force but reduce the effectiveness of this support while encouraging them in confronting the Athenians. For example, he told Tissaphernes that he was paying the sailors of the Peloponnesian fleet both too much and too regularly – claiming that his experience with the Athenian fleet made him an expert in these matters. Tissaphernes was quite happy to fall in with these suggestions, being currently disenchanted with both of the warring parties. He persisted, however, in forbidding the Peloponnesian fleet, which the king was financing through him, from attacking the Athenians in any of their strongholds, telling them to wait until they were reinforced by a Phoenician fleet, which was constantly being reported as being on the point of sailing.

Alcibiades' advice was, of course, much less even-handed than it appeared. Tissaphernes had no direct control over the Athenians, and the policy of allowing the two Hellenic powers to weaken each other, in practice, bore most heavily on the Peloponnesians, whose fleet had been sailing for an extended period and had suffered the usual deterioration of both ships and crews attendant on trireme forces – now exacerbated by the reduction in their pay. Alcibiades was, in fact, in his devious way, attempting to save the country of his birth from further disaster, preliminary to paving the way for a return to Athens.

Chapter 10
The Oligarchic Revolt

Aristotle, in his *Constitution of Athens*, describes the oligarchic revolt that briefly overthrew the Athenian democracy in 411 BC as follows: "As long as the fortunes of war were reasonably evenly balanced, the democracy was preserved, but when after the disaster of Sicily the Spartan side gained a considerable advantage because of their alliance with the king of Persia, the Athenians were forced to change their democracy into the regime of the Four Hundred." He elucidates his term 'forced' by explaining that "The decisive consideration in winning over the majority of the people was the belief that the king of Persia would be more likely to make a military alliance with them if their government was oligarchic."

Aristotle, as might be expected from one who was consistently derogatory of democracy, and particularly its demagogic leaders, goes to considerable lengths to present the revolt as the natural response of a number of responsible, meaning favouring oligarchy, citizens to the perilous situation of the state. The idea that the Great King would switch his alliance from the Spartans to the Athenians if the latter adopted an oligarchic government was the brain-child of Alcibiades, whose motives were still coloured by his desire for revenge on the democratic regime that had condemned him to death. And even if the idea had any scintilla of reality, it had little to do with 'winning over the majority,' who were actually intimidated into silence by the atmosphere of fear created by a number of assassinations of prominent supporters of the democracy and the packing of the assembly with armed youths who made it clear how the voting should go.

In fact, the revolt was initiated in Samos, where the great majority of the Athenians' forces, both land and marine, were currently stationed in support of the attempt to retain elements of the empire in the vicinity, which were being targeted by the Spartan/Persian alliance to secede. By some means, Alcibiades, now established as the chief advisor to Tissaphernes, the Persian satrap responsible for the area, was able to communicate a sufficiently persuasive message to the senior officers – generals and trierarchs – of the Athenian force at Samos to cause them to contemplate the overthrow of the democratic regime in Athens. Alcibiades' message expatiated on his ready access to the ear of the Great King (actually to his satrap Tissaphernes), by which he could persuade the king to form an alliance with the Athenians instead of the Spartans, thus shifting the balance of power as between Sparta and Athens decisively in favour of the latter. In order to achieve this desirable outcome, however, the Athenians would have to abandon their democracy in favour of an oligarchy, which would be much more to the taste of the king.

His message was received gladly by a significant number of the senior officers at Samos, many of whom would have naturally espoused the oligarchic cause, while at least initially, the rank and file of soldiers and sailors were unenthusiastic if not downright hostile. These latter were mollified by promises of high pay to be supplied by the Persian king, particularly as they had not been paid for some time. Eventually, a small group of the leading men travelled across to Asia to discuss the matter with Alcibiades. His powers of persuasion rapidly confirmed them with a firm conviction to take his message to Athens, particularly to animate the numerous *hetaireiai* – political clubs, largely of young, well-off men who were typically of an oligarchic cast – and so to sway the *ekklesia* to accept an oligarchic government. Accordingly, a deputation of envoys, amongst whom was Peisander, who was to become prominent in the oligarchic conspiracy, was sent to Athens.

The message that the envoys brought was short and brutal. Peisander portrayed in eloquent terms Athens' perilous state – threatened by the Peloponnesian fleet, which was bigger than the Athenians' and financially backed by the unlimited riches of the Great King. The only hope of salvation for the Athenians was an alliance with the Persians, and the key to persuading the king to switch his alliance from the Peloponnesians was the combination of the return of Alcibiades, with his influence on the Persians to Athens and the change of the government of Athens to an oligarchy. Initially, the *ekklesia* was distinctly hostile both to the thought of an oligarchic regime and the return of Alcibiades, but Peisander was able to persuade them to agree at least to the sending of a deputation led by himself to negotiate a possible alliance with Tissaphernes, with, it was assumed Alcibiades' assistance. Although they had not obtained an agreement for an oligarchy to be adopted, the deputation made the rounds of the *hetaireiai* to sow the seeds of the revolt before they left to travel to meet Tissaphernes. When it came to it, Alcibiades, being fully aware that Tissaphernes was highly unlikely to agree anything with the Athenians, for the Persians had not forgotten the humiliation inflicted on them by Kimon, but wishing to maintain the fiction that he controlled the satrap, effectively took the Persian side in the negotiations and demanded, apparently on behalf of the king, a series of conditions that he knew would be unacceptable to the Athenians with the aim of having them break off the talks. As he intended, the Athenian deputation left in high dudgeon and concluded both that Alcibiades could not bring about an alliance with Persia and also that he was unsuited to being a member of the oligarchic conspiracy.

Despite the collapse of the possibility of an alliance with Persia, which had supposedly been their major preoccupation, the oligarchic conspirators were unshaken in their commitment to ending democratic rule, having compromised themselves too far now to step back. Peisander and half of the rest of the conspirators from Samos returned, therefore, to Athens to bring about the installation of the oligarchy. Thucydides, in a manner reminiscent of the Old Oligarch, comments on the difficulty of overthrowing the democracy as a preamble to a passage praising the chief conspirators, naming

Peisander, Theramenes, Phrynichos and, in particular, Antiphon, a well-known *logographos,* a writer of speeches for those involved in legal cases. He maintains that destroying the freedoms that the people had had for half a century required abilities of a high order. In a different passage, he somewhat cuts the ground from beneath this argument, pointing out the insidious nature of the revolt, where no one could be sure of the views of the person to whom he was talking and where the expression of support for the democracy could well result in a premature and violent end, as exemplified by a number of assassinations of high-profile democrats, notably including Androcles, supposedly a demagogue who had been prominent in the passing of the death penalty on Alcibiades. In a society with few public means of communication, outside the *ekklesia* itself, and with a literacy rate of probably below twenty percent, the *demos* were reliant on word of mouth and rumour exaggerating the numbers of the conspirators, and a determined handful with a ready supply of violent youths and few qualms about using them was able rapidly to subdue the supposedly rock-solid support for the democracy.

Having thus prepared the ground, the conspirators published their proposals for the new regime, which declared that no one who was not on military service should be paid by the state – thus effectively excluding the *demos* from public office – and that the government should be restricted to five thousand of those who 'were best able to serve the state in person and with their money,' in other words, the aristocracy, the knights and the richest of the hoplite class. This 'rule of the five thousand' was a fictional piece of window dressing designed to obscure the fact that the real power was to lie in the hands of a select few, eventually revealed as the 'four hundred,' whose promise to consult the five thousand proved to be empty. For the moment, the *Boule* and *ekklesia* continued to be convoked but were completely under the control of the conspirators, who were able to propose motions to which there was no opposition. This situation culminated in the passing of a decree which created a board of ten commissioners who were to 'frame for the city the best constitution which they could devise, which would be laid before the people on a fixed day.'

When the day arrived, an assembly was summoned to meet at the temple of Poseidon, situated somewhat more than a mile outside the city walls – presumably as a disincentive for those who worked for a living to attend. Led by the ubiquitous Peisander, the assembly agreed on a number of resolutions, the first of which destroyed the cornerstone of the democratic constitution by abrogating and, in fact reversing the *graphe paranomon*, which exacted the death penalty for anyone attempting to introduce a resolution conflicting with existing laws – effectively a defence against attempts to subvert the democracy – which was, of course, entirely the intention of the oligarchs. Not only was the *graphe paranomon* abrogated, but anyone trying to apply it during the session was threatened with 'severe consequences,' which, according to Aristotle (Athenian Constitution, xxix, 4), meant execution. The list of resolutions continued with the abolishing of all existing magistracies and the payment of magistrates and also defined the procedure by which the oligarchic government was to be created. The procedure defined a nucleus of five individuals who were to choose a hundred, and each of the hundred was to co-opt three others, forming a governing body of four hundred. The selection process in each case was left to the individuals concerned and would obviously depend on personal relationships in each case, essentially providing a 'government of cronies' of like-minded friends and acquaintances. This Four Hundred were to meet in the chamber of the *Boule* of five hundred, which was to be abolished. They were to have absolute authority and might 'govern as they thought best.' The mythical Five Thousand were to be summoned whenever the Four Hundred chose – which in practice meant never.

At the subsequent meeting of the *ekklesia,* those not involved in the conspiracy were sent home, and the number of the conspirators was augmented by a number of foreigners and Athenian colonists, all of whom had been told to come armed. The Four Hundred then arrived, also with concealed weapons, together with 'a bodyguard of one hundred and twenty Hellenic youths whose services they used for any act of violence which they had in hand.' They then broke into the council chamber where the *Boule* of five hundred was sitting and told them to be gone, as their services were no longer required. The Four Hundred had brought with them the pay for the *Bouletai* for the remainder of their year of office, and as a contemptuous gesture, they were paid as they departed. (This, in

Thucydides VIII 69, is the only literary mention of payment for the members of the *Boule*). Having received no opposition either from the *ekklesia* or the *Boule*, as the result of the atmosphere of fear that the conspiracy had succeeded in creating, the Four Hundred took their place in the council chamber and began to rule, governing the city 'with a high hand,' with numerous imprisonments and executions of those they thought would be 'better out of the way.'

Having abandoned the forlorn hope of an alliance with the Persians, the Four Hundred decided to approach the Peloponnesian force at Decelea to explore the possibility of a peace settlement to end the war with Sparta. Accordingly, they sent heralds to Agis, the Spartan king in command. Agis, who was no doubt fully aware of the revolt in Athens, assumed that this was an admission of weakness and that the defences of the city would be in a chaotic state and sent for reinforcements from Sparta to undertake a full-scale assault. In the event, as his force approached the walls of Athens in a somewhat disorganised manner, it was met by a well-ordered defence involving cavalry and both light and heavy-armed infantry. Seeing his mistake, Agis ordered a retreat, but not before some of his more eager troops had been attacked and killed. On reaching the safety of Decelea, he promptly sent back the reinforcements to Sparta, with a typically Spartan reluctance to run the risk of losses of Sparta's most valuable and diminishing resource – her citizens. Despite this hostile, although unsuccessful, response to their overtures, the Four Hundred, a fair number of whom were probably 'Laconisers,' sympathetic to Sparta, continued to send envoys to Agis, who was now in a more receptive frame of mind. The pro-Spartan faction became more evident, with some envisaging direct Spartan support for the oligarchic administration.

At roughly the same time as the overthrow of the democracy in Athens, an oligarchic faction at Samos began to conspire against the democratic regime there, which had been installed after the revolution against the ruling class supported by both Athenian naval crews and the Athenian *demos*. The ever-present Peisander was sent to Samos to assure the conspirators, who followed the practice of numerical nomenclature, calling themselves the 'Three Hundred' of the support of the Four Hundred. Some of the leaders of the Athenian forces there also became involved, notably in the assassination of Hyperbolus, a demagogue who was ostracised by the Athenian *ekklesia* and went to Samos, presumably believing that the democratic regime there would provide some sort of protection for him. This anti-democratic development soon came to the ears of the Athenian sailors, who took violent exception to it and joined with the local democratic forces when they attacked the Three Hundred when they attempted to overthrow the democracy. Prominent among these were the *Paraloi*, the crew of the 'sacred ship' *Paralos*, who were all free-born Athenian citizens. Some thirty of the three hundred were killed in the fight; the three ring-leaders were banished, and the rest were forgiven and allowed to live under the democratic administration.

The pro-democratic Athenians on Samos then felt that the Athenian *demos* should be informed of the successful defence of the democracy on the island and sent Chaereas, one of their number, in the *Paralos* to apprise them, being unaware of the transfer of power to the Four Hundred. When the *Paraloi* arrived at Athens with the news, as might be expected, their reception was far from welcoming. Some of them were imprisoned, while the rest were transferred to a troop ship sent to keep watch on the island of Euboea – effectively a sort of marine house arrest. Chaereas, however, who seems to have been very quick on the uptake, slipped away and managed to return to Samos. Once returned to his comrades, he painted a lurid picture of the cruelty of the Four Hundred against the *demos* and, particularly, the relatives of the crews at Samos who were of the democratic faction, claiming that they were being imprisoned with the threat of execution if the fleet did not submit to the oligarchy's rule. (Parenthetically, whatever the truth of Chaereas' report, it does support the view that a significant proportion of the sailors at Samos were either Athenian citizens or were foreigners with familial ties to the city, rather than slaves or rootless mercenaries as some scholars have maintained.) Not unnaturally, the effect on the sailors was highly inflammatory, and there was a movement amongst them to attack those leaders of the recent oligarchic uprising who were still present. These were dissuaded, however, by a moderate faction who counselled against opening old wounds and creating chaos with the Peloponnesian fleet just over the horizon.

At this point, a significant individual enters the narrative: a trierarch named Thrasybulus, the son of Lycus. As a trierarch, he was a wealthy man, but unhesitatingly supported the democracy both in Samos and Athens. His importance extends beyond the oligarchic revolt, and he can fairly be described as a true hero of democracy, as well as a brave and successful naval commander. At the stage in the developments at Samos where the fleet was becoming aware of the overthrow of the democracy in Athens, Thrasybulus, together with a like-minded soldier Thrasyllus, thought the time was right for a proclamation of democracy amongst the Athenians at Samos, binding the soldiers and sailors with oaths to maintain democracy, to prosecute the war with the Peloponnesians, and to be enemies of the Four Hundred. They were joined by the native Samians of military age and together agreed to share their fortunes. The rank-and-file soldiers and sailors then called an assembly during which they dismissed any of their leaders – generals and trierarchs – who they suspected of oligarchic sympathies and elected new ones, amongst whom were Thrasybulus and Thrasyllus. They also raised the possibility of taking the empire into their own hands, based on Samos, 'as the city has revolted from us,' saying that they were in a position to compel the subject states to pay tribute to them as well as if they were sailing from the Piraeus.

Thrasybulus entertained a considerable respect for Alcibiades, possibly having been aware of his undoubted abilities as a military, and indeed naval, leader. He felt, therefore, that the cause of the democrats in Samos would be strengthened by support from Alcibiades, and he led a delegation to him while he was still established as Tissaphernes' advisor (an interesting example of the rules of warfare at the time, when Tissaphernes was bound by treaty to make war on Athenian forces, yet was able to receive an Athenian delegation, presumably with the usual mediation of heralds, who were universally held as untouchable.) Thrasybulus brought Alcibiades back to Samos, where he addressed the soldiers and sailors in an assembly. After having expressed his unhappiness at the injustice of his banishment and sentence of death, he painted in glowing terms the prospects for peace with the Persian king, citing his intimate relationship with Tissaphernes and the growing dissatisfaction between him and his supposedly allied Peloponnesians. So great was the confidence that Alcibiades inspired in his audience that the threat from the Peloponnesians was over that they clamoured to man the fleet and sail to the Piraeus immediately in order to bring down the Four Hundred and restore democracy to Athens, and they elected him as a general to lead them. Alcibiades was then forced to forbid absolutely this precipitate course of action; with characteristic persuasiveness, he managed to warn of the dangers of the enemy close at hand despite having played these down. In doing this, as Thucydides asserts, he 'appears to have done as eminent a service to the state as any man ever did,' as the proposed sailing against the oligarchy would have left Ionia and the Hellespont, through which the grain ships sailed to Athens, undefended against the large enemy force. Alcibiades then returned to the court of Tissaaphernes to continue his sedulous undermining of his alliance with the Peloponnesians. In fact, the alliance was already unravelling still further, with the Peloponnesians becoming ever more suspicious of Tissaphernes' double-dealing, which was exacerbated both by his niggardliness in supplying money and the news of Alcibiades' rehabilitation as an Athenian general. The Spartan admiral Astyochus had also dealt ham-fistedly with a minor mutiny amongst the Syracusan crews in his fleet, who protested about their lack of pay and was only saved from a more serious outbreak by being replaced by another Spartan, Mindarus.

After hearing from the crew of the *Paralos* of the strong commitment to democracy of the Athenian forces at Samos and their antagonism to the oligarchic revolt, the Four Hundred had dispatched ten commissioners to Samos to try to calm their fears and bring them around to supporting their administration. Their journey had been delayed en route after their hearing of the vehemence of the democratic sentiment expressed by the soldiers and sailors, but they had eventually arrived during Alcibiades' sojourn at Samos. They were permitted to address an assembly and attempted to convince their hearers of the falsity of Chaereas' stories of atrocities against their families, and they claimed that the Five Thousand were to be established as the true rulers rather than the Four Hundred. Whether due to a lack of persuasive eloquence or perhaps underlying disbelief in their own cause, the assembly grew ever more angry and unwilling to listen to them, and eventually, Alcibiades had to step in and use his power over the *ochlos* (mob) to allow the commissioners to escape with their lives; he dismissed them with the message that the Four Hundred must be got rid of, and whatever regime ruled Athens, they must be steadfast against the Peloponnesian threat.

Alcibiades' message to the Four Hundred, communicated to them by the returning commissioners, had the effect of widening the split between the extreme oligarchs, notably including Antiphon, Peisander and Phrynichos, and the moderates, of whom Theramenes was the leader. The extremists, being resolutely against any softening of the revolt, were unprepared to accept Alcibiades' stipulations, and rather than maintaining the war against the Peloponnesians, decided to ask for Spartan assistance in keeping them in power, Antiphon and Phrynichos being sent to Sparta for that purpose, an action that outraged popular opinion in Athens, and further eroded the moderates' commitment to the revolt. The growing antagonism against the extreme faction was heightened by their fortification of the mole of the Piraeus, known as Eetionia, which formed one side of the entrance to the harbour. The purpose of the fortification, which was being carried out by a detachment of hoplites, was obviously to provide a choke point by which entrance to the harbour could be controlled. The originators of the scheme claimed that it was intended to prevent any attempt by the anti-oligarchic fleet from Samos from mounting an invasion from the Piraeus; however, Theramenes maintained that its purpose was the even more sinister one of allowing the Peloponnesian fleet and land forces access to Athens.

Theramenes' suspicions and the humiliation of the envoys who had gone to Sparta to sue for peace and returned empty-handed appear to have eroded the hold that the Four Hundred had established over the Athenian citizenry, as evidenced by a number of anti-oligarchy incidents. The first was the assassination of Phrynichos, one of the leaders of the extreme faction of the Four Hundred who had just returned from Sparta, who was very publicly attacked in the marketplace by a member of the border guard. Another was the capture and imprisonment of Alexicles, an oligarchic general, by the hoplites who were working on the fortification of the Eetionea. This put the Four Hundred into a state of panic. Some of their number were for arming themselves and setting out to the rescue of Alexicles, but they were dissuaded by Theramenes, who undertook to go to try to free him without initiating a conflict, seeing that the incident had fomented a highly dangerous state of excitement in the city and the Piraeus. When he spoke to the soldiers, he adopted an authoritarian tone, which had no effect on them, and they were concerned to question him on the purpose of the fortifications on which they were working and suggesting that they would be better employed in demolishing them. Theramenes, who, of course, had perpetrated the idea that the works were intended to ease the entry of the enemy into Athens, was happy to go along with the suggestion, although unwilling to make his acquiescence too obvious, saying that if the hoplites thought it best to demolish them, then he thought so too. With that, the hoplites and a crowd of men from the Piraeus got onto the new fortifications and began to pull them down, calling on those around to come and help them if they wished to end the rule of the Four Hundred. On the next day, when the demolition was complete and having freed Alexicles, the hoplites marched into the city, taking up a position in the temple of Castor and Pollux. Here, they were visited by members of the Four Hundred, who tried to calm them with promises to establish the 'Five Thousand' as the ruling body, to which the Four Hundred would be responsible. The soldiers were eventually mollified and departed with the agreement that there would be an assembly on a specified date to deliberate 'on the restoration of harmony.'

The atmosphere of peace and reconciliation prevailing on the day fixed for the assembly was rudely shattered by the sight of forty-two Peloponnesian ships led by the Spartan king Agesandridas sailing along the coast of Salamis, the island directly opposite the Piraeus. In fact, they were sailing to Euboea, the large island to the East of Athens, at the invitation of the inhabitants, who wished to take advantage of Athens' enfeebled state to end her domination over them. Initially, the Athenian citizens were convinced that the Peloponnesian squadron was headed for the Piraeus to fulfil Theramenes' prediction of an invasion, and panicked preparations were made to man what ships there were to confront an attack, with 'the whole city' rushing down to the Piraeus, 'thinking that a conflict with their enemies more serious than their domestic strife was now awaiting them... at the very mouth of the harbour.'

The Peloponnesian ships sailed on towards Euboea, however, and the Athenians' concern then became that of preventing them from fomenting a revolt in the island, and hurriedly despatched a fleet manned, according to Thucydides, by crews, 'not yet trained to work together,' one of the few examples in the literature where the need for the crews to be trained is mentioned. This fleet joined with some ships that had been stationed off Euboea, made up of thirty-six ships, which set off in pursuit of the Peloponnesians. Perhaps in view of the haste in which the fleet had been assembled and the inexperience of the crews, it is not surprising that in the subsequent battle, they were heavily defeated, with the loss of twenty-two ships with their crews who were either killed or taken prisoner. Following their victory, the Peloponnesians went on to induce the Euboeans to revolt, threatening the Athenians' supply of grain, which was transported by ship close to the island.

The effect of this demarche on the Athenian citizenry was more drastic even than that of the terrible disaster at Sicily. That had happened at the extremity of the civilised world as far as they were concerned. This disaster was on their own doorstep and left them with the Piraeus empty of ships, and even if they had them, there were no crews to man them. The fleet and army at Samos were disaffected and talking of basing themselves there permanently as a separate democratic state. And a victorious Peloponnesian fleet was surely about to take advantage of Athens' further debilitation. In the face of all this, some semblance of the democratic spirit emerged, resulting in many meetings of the full assembly on the historical venue of Pnyx Hill. These assemblies were no longer cowed by the *haiteirai* but still lacked the confidence to re-establish the democratic regime that had been overthrown. The rule of the Four Hundred was terminated and replaced by that of the 'Five Thousand,' while specially appointed *nomothetai* devised and established a new constitution. The people also voted to recall Alcibiades and to re-establish good relations with the forces at Samos.

Some of the leaders of the extreme faction of the oligarchy, including Peisander and Alexicles, 'stole away' to the Spartan garrison at Decelea, while others, notably Antiphon, stayed to face trial. Antiphon, according to Thucydides, gave a brilliant speech in his defence, but to no avail: he was condemned and executed.

As far as Thucydides was concerned, this was the end of the oligarchic revolt, and the major cause of its failure was 'that the Athenian sailors would be impatient of the oligarchical system, and that disaffection would start at Samos and end in their [the oligarchs'] overthrow.'

Chapter 11
The Restored Democracy

The oligarchic revolt leading to the rule of the Four Hundred had shaken the apparently rock-solid Athenian democracy, and even though the Four Hundred, weakened by internal dissension, the counter-revolt at Eetionia, and the defeat at sea followed by the loss of Euboea, offered no resistance to their dismissal, it was some time before the radical democracy was re-established. The *demos* had temporarily lost its confidence, and it took a succession of naval victories to re-vitalise the democratic spirit for the emergence of at least one demagogue, Cleophon, to rally an overwhelming support for democracy. The major figure in this renaissance was the ubiquitous Alcibiades, whose abilities as a naval commander did much to restore the confidence of the Athenians, and the prosecution of the war with Sparta went well, for a time at least, seeing the Spartans sue for peace twice. This superiority was not to last, however, and the increasing influence of the Persians, or rather their money, together with an able Spartan admiral, Lysander, eventually led, with the assistance both of bad decisions in the Athenian *ekklesia* and possibly treachery by the oligarchic faction, to disaster and the overthrow of the democracy again in 404 BC.

After the overthrow of the Four Hundred by an assembly that met on the Pnyx, it was agreed that the administration should be in the hands of those who could furnish themselves with arms, who would be known as 'the five thousand,' resurrecting the idea that was supposedly the objective of the original oligarchic revolt, but which was honoured in the breach by the Four Hundred. The leading light in the establishment of this constitution was Theramenes, who was from the moderate end of the oligarchic spectrum and who had supported the revolt in the hopes of achieving, as he saw it, a constitution containing elements both of democracy and oligarchy. In fact, forbidding payment for public office holders fell far short of the inclusive democracy that had prevailed prior to the revolt, effectively excluding those without private means from office. Perhaps unsurprisingly, both Thucydides and Aristotle, who were both unenthusiastic about democracy, particularly in its more radical form, praise the rule of the Five Thousand, the former calling it, 'During its early days the best that the Athenians ever enjoyed within my memory.' As it excluded the *thetes*, however, and thus the common sailors of the fleet, it was never representative of those most involved in the war and was doomed to be short-lived.

The Peloponnesian fleet under its new Spartan admiral Mindarus lost patience with Tissaphernes, who had continued to follow Alcibiades' advice to be parsimonious in his supply of money, and decided to accept the invitation of Pharnabazus, the other coastal satrap, to base themselves in the Hellespont. Pharnabazus promised to support them actively, and he was as good as his word. The Peloponnesians, however, were attacked by an Athenian force commanded by the two democratic leaders of the fleet at Samos, Thrasybulus and Thrasyllus, at Cynossema. The battle commenced with the Peloponnesians in an extended line, which the Athenians attempted to outflank, weakening their centre as they did so, and the Peloponnesians scored an initial success breaking through the centre, at which they assumed victory was theirs and began to celebrate, losing their formation as they did so. At this, Thrasybulus, who was leading the right wing, obscured by the rocky promontory of Cynossema, brought his ships around to attack the now disorganised enemy and secured the victory. Although the margin in terms of ships destroyed or captured was not great (twenty-two to fifteen), this victory heartened the Athenians, as did the recovery of nearby Cyzicus, which had revolted by the fleet having, which had rapidly repaired their ships. The Athenians also met with success shortly after at Abydus, also in the Hellespont, where Alcibiades arrived during the engagement with eighteen ships, tipping the balance towards the Athenians, who captured thirty enemy ships. Alcibiades had also extracted a large amount of money from the Carian city of Halicarnassus and installed an Athenian governor on Cos. He also claimed that he had made Tissaphernes a still greater friend of Athens. Some doubt was cast on this claim when, during the following winter, he took a single trireme 'bearing friendly offerings and gifts' to visit Tissaphernes and cement their relationship even further.

Tissaphernes, however, who was extremely displeased by the Peloponnesians' switch of loyalty to his rival Pharnabazus, for which he probably held Alcibiades at least partly to blame, was in no mood for pleasantries and arrested Alcibiades and imprisoned him. It will come as no surprise that Alcibiades managed to provide himself with a horse and escaped after a month's incarceration.

After the winter, Mindarus attempted to re-take Cyzicus with his Peloponnesian fleet and a land army supplied by Pharnabazus. They were confronted by an Athenian fleet of three squadrons led by Alcibiades, Thrasybulus and Theramenes, which had managed to elude the enemy's scouts and took Mindarus by surprise. The result was a crushing defeat for the Peloponnesians in which Mindarus was killed, according to some reports actually by Alcibiades. Apart from its significance in the context of the war, the battle is famous for a message from Mindarus' second in command to the Spartan government, which was intercepted by the Athenians and which came to be established as the defining example of 'laconic' – from Laconia, the Greek province where Sparta was situated. The message read: 'Admiral dead, ships lost, men starving, don't know what to do.'

The victory at Cyzicus emboldened the democratic party at Athens, who continued to be encouraged by the steadfast adherence to democracy by the fleet at Samos to overcome Theramenes' Rule of the Five Thousand. Their leader was Cleophon, cast in the same mould as Cleon and Hyperbolus. The democratic regime was restored, with payment for holders of public office, and augmented by the 'Two-obol payment' or one-sixth of a drachma per diem, originated by Cleophon, which seems to have been a general disbursement to the indigent – of which there were many following the interruption of the imperial tribute, soon to be re-imposed, and the isolation of the silver mines. Cleophon also reintroduced the employment of the poor in public works, first initiated by Pericles, including the building of a new temple of Athene at the Acropolis.

Cleophon also persuaded the assembly to reject a peace overture from the Spartans after Cyzicus, offering to vacate Decelea and cease hostilities. In this, he was no doubt echoing the views of the fleet, as the offer would have left the Spartans with their considerable gains in Ionia, and while the fleet under the command of Alcibiades had won a series of victories and showed every sign of dominating the Peloponnesian force. Cleophon, as a demagogue, receives a very poor press from Xenophon and Plutarch (probably simply repeating him). Referred to as 'the lyre-maker,' also by Aristophanes, in the same way that Cleon is referred to as 'the tanner' and Hyperbolus as 'the lamp-maker.' These are all attempts to portray the demagogues as 'men of the people' – *thetes,* in fact – where certainly Cleon was the son of a wealthy owner of a tanning business and was probably a member of the *hippeis*, and so similarly was Cleophon. Xenophon and Plutarch agree that Cleophon made his successful speech urging the assembly to reject the Spartan peace offer when he was 'drunk and wearing his breastplate.' The fact that he owned a breastplate made him at least one of the hoplite class rather tends to undermine the picture of him as a guttersnipe.

The Athenian control over the Hellespont became so complete that the Athenians were able to establish a toll station at Chrysopolis, supported by a garrison of thirty ships and two generals, at which ships coming from the Euxine Sea were obliged to pay one-tenth of the value of their freight. This, together with the re-taking of Thasos and Selymbria, with their tribute payments, laid the basis for a recovery of the city's finances, although these never achieved the level of that at the height of the empire. Alcibiades also took Byzantium, helped by anti-Spartan forces in the city, which was strategically sited at the Eastern end of the Hellespont and thus important for the supply route for Athens' grain.

Alcibiades' military achievements, which underpinned the ever-more confident democratic regime, were such as to create a popular demand for him to return to Athens some eight years (407 BC) after his banishment. After some trepidation, he agreed to return and, though welcomed generally, arrived on the day the Athenians celebrated *Plynteria* when the statue of Athene was veiled – taken by some as an ill-omen. However, his generalship was recognised by a decree giving him full powers for the conduct of the war, essentially making him commander-in-chief. At the same time, he was solemnly freed from the curse that was laid on him (probably mistakenly) as 'profaner of the Eleusinian rites.' In a fine stroke of irony, he re-established the annual procession along the sacred way to the Eleusinian shrine, which had been prevented by the Spartan occupation of Decelea, which he had done so much to promote.

Plutarch suggests that the eagerness with which Alcibiades was put in charge of the war was motivated, at least in some quarters, by the fear that he might entertain despotic aspirations, there certainly being no shortage of people advising him to become a tyrant. It was felt that the safest place for him was on the poop of a warship directing warfare against the Spartans rather than participating in the political life of the city.

Alcibiades' successes led the *demos* to develop unreasonable expectations of their continuation. As Plutarch says, 'If ever a man was ruined by his own glory, it was Alcibiades.' There was murmuring, encouraged by one Thrasybulus, not the trierarch but a demagogic enemy of Alcibiades, when, with a fleet of 100 ships, he attacked the inhabitants of Andros and the Spartans who were supporting them and won a victory but did not take the city. The Athenian *demos* 'never considered how extremely money was wanted and that, having to carry on a war with an enemy who had supplies of all things from a Great King, he was often forced to quit his armament in order to obtain money and provisions for the subsistence of his soldiers.' This was brought to a head when a new Spartan admiral, Lysander, was sent as a replacement for Mindarus. He had established a close relationship with the Persian King Darius' son Cyrus, who provided Lysander with a large sum of money (500 Talents, with the promise of more if necessary, even if this meant melting down his throne, which was made of gold and silver), enabling him to pay his sailors four obols a day, where Alcibiades could hardly afford three.

When the Athenian and Peloponnesian fleets were lying close to each other near Notion, Alcibiades took the opportunity of a reluctance on the part of Lysander to engage with the Athenians to go to Caria in a quest for more money. He left the fleet in the care of the steersman (effectively the captain) of his ship, a man named Antiochus, giving him strict instructions not to engage with the enemy. Antiochus, however, being of a headstrong nature, ignored the instruction and, with his and another ship, sailed 'close by the prows' of Lysander's fleet in a foolhardy piece of coat-trailing. Lysander dispatched a couple of ships after them initially, but then, seeing that more of the Athenian fleet was following, ordered his entire fleet also to engage and defeated the Athenians, who lost fifteen ships, and Antiochus lost his life. Although this was a comparatively trivial affair, it confirmed the gathering disenchantment with Alcibiades in the Athenian demos, who felt almost certainly unjustly that 'he had lost the ships through neglect of duty and dissolute conduct' and he was voted off the board of generals. Alcibiades never returned to Athens after this and retired to a castle on the Hellespont, which he had provided as a refuge for himself, doubtless aware of the fickleness of the *demos* towards even the most successful of its heroes. As a result of this bizarre episode, the Athenians lost undoubtedly their most talented military commander. Konon became the commander in chief of the navy in his stead.

By one of those inexplicable decisions that typified the Spartan conduct of the war, Lysander, who had been very successful in getting the Peloponnesian fleet into a formidable state of battle-worthiness, was replaced by a new admiral, Callicratidas. The new man was not received with universal acclaim, with friends of Lysander questioning the wisdom of replacing their man when he had established himself as a successful commander. Plutarch also suggests that his friends had an ulterior motive in this, arising from Lysander's rather strangely divided character: being personally incorruptible but notorious for showering his friends with honours and riches in a most un-Spartan way. There was no doubt of his military abilities, however. Lysander did not help matters by claiming, as he handed over the fleet to Callicratidas, that he did so as 'master of the sea and victor in battle.' Callicratidas faced down his critics by inviting anyone of the Spartans under his command who doubted his abilities to raise their objections to him, and he would sail back to Sparta and report what the conditions in the fleet were. No one dared to question the order of the Spartan administration.

For a time, they were highly successful under their new admiral, taking a fortress in Chios and the city of Methymna in Lesbos. Callicratidas then issued a challenge to Konon, whose fleet was also off Lesbos, telling him that 'he would put a stop to his playing the wanton with his bride, the sea.' Konon, whose forces had been reduced to seventy ships, attempted to escape to Samos but was forced into a battle outside Mytilene and was defeated with the loss of thirty ships, with the rest being beached and blockaded in the harbour there. That this was a desperate situation was recognised by the Athenians, who exerted every effort, including the melting down of gold and silver dedications in the temples of the Acropolis, to supply the necessary expenditure. Eventually, they managed to assemble a fleet of 110 triremes to go to the relief of Konon, 'Putting aboard all those of military age, whether slave or free. Even the knights went aboard in considerable numbers.' The fact that members of the hippeis – the second highest of the Solonic classes – deigned to man the ships hitherto seen as floating sinks of proletarian effort – illustrates the degree of alarm that had seized the entire population. At Samos, they collected more ships to reach a total of more than 150.

When Callicratidas heard that the Athenian relief force was already at Samos, he took 120 ships from the blockade at Mytilene, leaving fifty, and moved to a position opposite the Arginusai islands. At much the same time, the Athenians reached the islands, which lie opposite Mytilene, where they moored for the night. Seeing the Athenians' fires at night, Callicratidas decided to attack them at midnight, but his plans were disrupted by a storm with heavy rain and thunder and his sallying forth to attack was delayed until daybreak, thus losing the element of surprise he had hoped for. When the Athenians saw him, they 'stood out to meet him' in a somewhat complex formation with two wings doubled up in places, apparently to protect some of the ships with scratch crews, who could not be expected to match the Peloponnesians, in an effort to prevent their line being broken. By contrast, the Peloponnesians were arranged in a single line, with each ship intended to execute a *diplous* manoeuvre, penetrating the Athenian line and encircling them.

Callicratidas' steersman, Hermon the Megarian, urged him to avoid battle and to sail away, seeing that the Athenians' numerical advantage was so great, but Callicratidas said, 'That Sparta would fare no worse if he were killed, but flight would be a disgrace,' reflecting perhaps a lack of appreciation of the strategic importance of the forthcoming encounter. The fight that ensued was a long one, in which the carefully arranged formations were rapidly lost. At a significant point, Callicratidas' ship rammed an enemy, but he had failed to brace himself against the shock and fell overboard, never to be seen again. This was followed by the defeat of the Peloponnesian left wing by Protomachus leading the Athenian right, at which the Peloponnesians began to flee from the contest. At the end, the Athenian losses were twenty-five ships with their crews. On the Peloponnesian side, the Spartans lost all but one of their ten ships and more than sixty of their allies.

After the victory, it was decided that Theramenes and Thrasybulus, both trierarchs and ex-generals, with some others, should sail with forty-seven ships to the aid of the disabled Athenian vessels and their crews, many of which would be clinging to floating wreckage while the rest sailed to Mytilene to attack the remaining blockading force, which was led by Eetonicus. These plans were disrupted, however, by the advent of a violent storm, and the rescue attempt was called off – a decision with profound after-effects.

Eetonicus learnt of the heavy defeat when a dispatch boat returned to report the result of the battle. In a blatant piece of news management, he sent the boat out again, telling the crew to deck the boat with garlands and to return with news of Callicratidas' comprehensive victory, with every Athenian ship destroyed. He then ordered the ships manning the blockade to sail to Chios and led his land forces back to Methymna, leaving Konon free to launch his ships.

The news of the abandonment of the shipwrecked crews appears to have arrived even before that of the victory itself, and the generals who had taken part in the battle were deposed and summoned to Athens to give an account of their actions. Two of them, Protomachus and Aristogenes, did not return. The six who did were: Pericles (the son of the great statesman), Diomedon, Lysias, Aristocrates, Thrasyllus (one of the heroes of the 411 revolt) and Erasinides. The action against the generals began with an individual case brought against Erasinides by Archedamus, a demagogue, in one of the law courts. The charge was that Erasinides had embezzled money from the Hellespont, which was rightly due to the people and also of misconduct as a general. The court decreed that Erasinides should be imprisoned. After this, the five remaining generals made a statement before the *Boule* with regard to the battle and the violence of the storm, but this evoked no sympathy from the hearers, and a motion that they should be imprisoned was also passed. In a subsequent meeting of the assembly, Theramenes, who had been one of those charged with undertaking the rescue, took over the attack on the generals, presumably to deflect criticism from himself and his fellow trierarchs.

When the generals were given a (brief) chance to speak, they maintained that they had assigned the task of rescue to men, such as Theramenes and Thrasybulus, who were both trierarchs and ex-generals and so they could not be held responsible. They also refused to calumniate the trierarchs, saying that the cause of the disaster was the storm that prevented the operation. They produced witnesses from the ships' companies to corroborate their narrative. After this, the assembly appeared to accept their claim. However, the meeting was adjourned as it was late in the day, and the raised hands could not have been seen for counting. It was agreed that the *Boule* would bring in a proposal regarding the manner in which the generals should be tried. Immediately afterward, the festival of *Apaturia,* 'at which fathers and kinsmen meet together,' was celebrated. According to Xenophon, Theramenes arranged for the attendance of a 'large number' of men wearing mourning clothes and with their hair cut short – another sign of mourning – claiming that they were relatives of those who had perished; also Callixeinus, a demagogue, was bribed to accuse the generals in the *Boule*.

Callixeinous' intervention was apparently successful, and the proposal of the *Boule*, drafted by him, declared that the assembly had heard the testimony of the generals and others, and so without delay, the assembly should vote on the guilt of the generals for 'not picking up the men who won the victory in the naval battle.' If found guilty, they should be 'handed over to the Eleven (being the committee of magistrates who directed public executions) and executed, and their property confiscated.' Some of those present recognised that this proposal was both unjust, in that the generals had not been allowed time to present their defence and also that the trying of the whole group together conflicted with a principle formulated by Cannonus, which prescribed that each individual should be tried separately, and so was unconstitutional, and should be subject to the *Graphe Paranomon*. Euryptolemus attempted to bring forward a summons on Callixeinus, but this was howled down by the mob, and Lyciscus moved that anyone attempting to apply the *Graphe Paranomon* should be judged by the same vote as the generals, a proposal which received shouts of approval. Some of the Prytanes, who managed the voting for individual tribes, refused initially to go ahead with the vote, and Callixeinus again used the threat of inclusion in the vote on the generals to intimidate them into putting the question. The only exception was Socrates, who said that in no case would he act except in accordance with the law, a stand that he mentioned in his Apologia when he was under the threat of execution himself.

Before the vote took place, Euryptolemos addressed the assembly again, speaking as a kinsman of Pericles, one of the generals. He urged that the men should be tried according to the decree of Cannonus, i.e., individually, and that each man should be given time to make his defence.

He pointed out that Aristarchus, an oligarch who had 'destroyed the democracy' and had betrayed the Athenian outpost at Oenoe to the Thebans at the end of the revolt, had been granted his full legal rights in his trial, while Callixeinus' proposal denied these men their rights, despite their having won a great victory. He proposed that a vote should be taken as to determining whether the men should be tried under the decree of Cannonus or together in a single vote, as demanded by Callixeinus. The vote was taken, and the decision was in favour of Euryptolemos, but an objection was raised by Menecles, and a second vote was taken. This time, the decision was for Callixeinus' proposal, as backed by the *Boule*. The assembly then voted on the guilt of the eight generals and found them jointly guilty; they were then condemned to death, and the six present were executed.

As Euryptolemos had predicted, the Athenians soon repented of their decision and, in characteristic fashion, turned against those who had 'misled' them, notably the leading light in the prosecution, Callixeinus. He and others were to be brought to trial, but according to Xenophon, they escaped during a 'factional disturbance.'

The mob mentality that had taken over the assembly had illustrated that the safeguards supposedly protecting the constitution, which formed the foundation of the democracy, could be set aside by one or two individuals borne along by a short-lived but powerful surge of probably misplaced emotion. The *demos* rapidly came to believe that the wrecked crews, with whom they identified as fellow *thetes*, had been abandoned by their generals –

the only identifiable upper class recognised by the democracy. The facts of the storm, the contributory responsibility of the trierarchs – also part of the upper class – and those such as the fact that at least one of those executed had actually been wrecked and saved himself and had hardly been in a position to lead the rescue attempt, were lost in the urgent need to find scapegoats. Unfortunately, those that were found were experienced naval commanders whose loss seriously depleted the strength of the navy.

It might be suggested that the very reliance of the Athenian fleet on the *demos*, whilst in many ways providing a powerful, cohesive force uniting the citizenry of all classes, rendered it vulnerable to occasional outbreaks of irrationality in the *ekklesia*, which maintained a proprietorial view of the navy, and particularly of those who rowed the ships. The thought that 'our boys' had been left to drown by upper-class officers after defeating the enemy was incendiary. But no such sentiment exercised the Spartan equivalent (admittedly, not a democratic institution) at the very real disaster that had overcome the Peloponnesian fleet, which was manned by mercenaries. The Spartan government, of course, recognised the severity of their defeat and, as after Cyzicus, sued for peace with the same offer of a withdrawal of their forces from Decelea and everything else left as it was. Again, Cleophon led the resistance to this in the *ekklesia*, and it was rejected.

Following the defeat of the Peloponnesian fleet, the remnants who had escaped to Chios with Eetonicus' ships were left in dire straits. Winter was coming on, and there was no money to pay the crews. The sailors, for a time, found work in the fields of the Chian farmers, but this ended as winter took hold. They were driven by starvation to contemplate a coup against the Chians, but this was discovered and nipped in the bud by Eetonicus. Eventually, he sent a plea to Sparta to re-establish Lysander as admiral. Formally speaking, he could not be reappointed, as it was forbidden for an admiral to serve twice, so he was appointed as vice-admiral with the tacit understanding that he, and not the admiral, was in charge.

Lysander quickly re-established his close friendship with Cyrus, son of the Persian king Darius, who gave him a large sum of money. Then Darius became seriously ill, and Cyrus was summoned to his bedside, but not before he had put Lysander in charge of his satrapy and authorised to receive the tribute money from it. He then set about reversing the Athenians' fortunes along the Ionian coast and Islands. The Athenian fleet under Konon caught up with him at Ephesus, but he refused to come out to fight, and the Athenians went elsewhere to continue their own harrying of the Ionian coast. The Athenians had strengthened their fleet and had appointed a further three generals, including Tydea, to lead it – surely making it somewhat over-generalled. Eventually, Lysander entered the Hellespont, intending to disrupt the passage of the ships that maintained Athens' grain supply. He besieged the port city of Lampsacus, which was allied to Athens. Hearing this, Konon sailed to the area but arrived after

Lampsacus had fallen to the Peloponnesians, providing them with a wealth of booty and supplies.

The Athenian fleet then provisioned at Sestos, on the opposite bank of the Hellespont and somewhat to the West of it, then sailed on to a position opposite Lampsacus, an open beach with no harbourage called Aigospotamoi 'Goat's rivers,' where they anchored. On the next day, Lysander ordered his men to embark the fleet and to get ready for battle, but also that no one should move or put out. At daybreak, the Athenian fleet sailed to form a line of battle at the mouth of the harbour, but the Peloponnesian ships remained in the harbour, and the Athenians eventually gave up late in the day and sailed back to Aegospotamoi. Lysander had the Athenians followed by scout boats to report on their movements. This scenario was repeated on three successive days, with the Athenians offering battle and Lysander's fleet staying put.

During these four days, Alcibiades, having observed them from his castle, which by an amazing coincidence overlooked the beach, rode down to advise the Athenians that their choice of anchorage was a poor one, being both exposed and remote from any source of supplies – the nearest being at Sestos, some two miles away. He advised them to return to Sestos and anchor in the harbour, where they were protected. There were plentiful supplies on hand and was close enough to enable them to attack the enemy as they wished. This message was received neither gratefully nor courteously by the generals, particularly the recently appointed ones, especially Tydea, who told him to be off as they were in command now. Alcibiades, having performed his final service to his native city, galloped away, as Plutarch says, 'Suspecting treachery.' The Athenians remained at Aigospotamoi, and the crews got into the habit of walking over to Sestos for provisions after their ships had anchored following a fruitless day's waiting for the Peloponnesians to come out.

On the fifth day, the routine was followed again, with the difference that Lysander ordered the scout boats to ascertain that the Athenians had disembarked and were scattered over the coast and then to return displaying a shield (another version has them reflecting the sun with a polished shield). And, as Xenophon remarks: 'They did just as he had ordered.' Then Lysander ordered the entire Peloponnesian fleet of some 200 ships to sail with all speed to the Athenian anchorage. Konon, the Athenian commander-in-chief, saw the oncoming attack and attempted to signal to his men to return to their ships, but they were too widely scattered. His own ship, and seven others with him, were fully manned, and recognising the disaster that awaited if he tarried, sailed immediately for the open sea with the sacred ship *Paralos*. The rest were caught unprepared, most of them either undermanned or empty of their crews. There was no battle. Those on the ships were taken prisoner immediately, and most on the shore were rounded up, with a few escaping. Konon, realising that to return to Athens bearing news of this disaster would result in his immediate arrest, 'trial' and execution, sent the *Paralos* to carry the news to Athens, while he sailed away with eight ships to seek refuge with Euagoras in Cyprus, pausing only to put in at Abarnia, the promontory of Lampsacus to seize the cruising sails that Lysander's ships had left before the attack on the Athenians (this was standard practice for triremes before a battle). By doing this, he lessened the likelihood of pursuit. It might be wondered how Konon knew the whereabouts of the sails.

According to Xenophon, Lysander took several thousand prisoners, including the generals Adeimantos and Philocles, to Lampsacus, where he discussed their fate with his allies. There was much ill feeling against the Athenians for a number of 'outrages,' including an incident when two triremes from the Peloponnesian fleet had been captured and their crews thrown overboard by the order of Philocles. They were also indignant regarding a vote in the Athenian *ekklesia* in favour of cutting off the right hand of every man taken alive, a decree supported by Philocles, who is referred to as a demagogue by Plutarch (it does not actually seem to have been put into practice). It was decided that all the Athenian prisoners would be put to death, some three or four thousand of them, with the exception of Adeimantos, who had opposed the decree in the ekklesia. Perhaps inevitably, Adeimantos was suspected of 'betraying the fleet.' In another recounting of the episode, Philocles was the only Athenian to be put to death, and the subject is still the object of academic debate.

The disaster of Aigospotamoi raises a number of questions. Why was the fleet so apparently out of control of the commander-in-chief, whose ship and those of some others close by were ready to sail, while all the others were left under or unmanned? Were the newly appointed generals unwilling to accept his leadership? Were there no voices raised against the folly of leaving their ships unattended, with the enemy 'just around the corner'? Could it possibly have been a conspiracy by oligarchic sympathisers, who perhaps thought, with justification as it later turned out, that a bloodless victory for Lysander would result in his coming to an agreement with the Athenian oligarchs, to install an oligarchic regime in Athens? The deaths of thousands of *thetes*, if it happened, might not have been predicted and, in any case, might well have been regarded as of little importance, or indeed a useful diminution of democratic support in Athens. While there is no doubt that Konon was to become a significant supporter of democracy, his escape to Cyprus has the suggestion of a previously devised plan.

When the *Paralos* reached Athens with the news, it was greeted by universal horror and fear, with the populace all too able to imagine the fate that awaited them, with their memories of the way in which their forces had treated vanquished cities such as Melos and Mytilene. It was a night when 'no man slept, and the sound of wailing filled the streets.' Meanwhile, Lysander and his fleet undertook a fairly leisurely progress towards Athens, pausing first to eject the Athenian garrison at Byzantium and return the city to Spartan control. As the journey continued, he rounded up the Athenians on every island and gave them safe conduct, provided they returned to Athens. His intention was for the city to become overcrowded so as to be more vulnerable to blockade. He stationed his fleet off the Piraeus, preventing any merchant ship from entering. At the same time, Pausanias, the other Spartan king, advanced to the hinterland of Athens, while Agis came down from Decelea from the other direction, and so Athens was completely blockaded by land and sea, with the supply chains on which it was so dependent completely cut off. Despite this desperate situation, the *ekklesia* maintained an attitude of defiance, even going so far as to imprison one of its number who argued for suing for peace. Eventually, as the effects of the blockade became more apparent, it was agreed that an embassy would be sent to Sparta to offer a peace settlement, which included Athens becoming an ally of Sparta, relinquishing her empire while retaining the walls of the Piraeus, her fleet, and the long walls. The details of these proposals reached the ears of the Ephors before the envoys, who were told to go back to Athens before they even arrived in Sparta and to come back only if they carried an offer which recognised Athens' weak position.

The Athenians were taken aback at this and at a loss as to what to propose. Then Theramenes, the oligarch who had been instrumental in the execution of the generals, came forward to volunteer to see Lysander in person to discover whether there was any hope of saving the walls. He spent three months with Lysander, claiming to have been 'held' by him, but according to Xenophon, merely waiting for the effects of the blockade to become critical so as to soften up the *ekklesia* to accept the Spartan terms. He then returned to Athens, saying that Lysander had claimed that he did not have the authority to sign any peace agreement – that only the ephors could do that.

Theramenes was then appointed as the lead negotiator with ten men to go to Sparta to discover what were the requirements for a peace agreement.

The Spartans then held a convocation of their allies to see what Athens' fate should be. The Thebans and Corinthians argued for the total destruction of the city and the selling of its inhabitants into slavery. Their animus is perhaps understandable in being neighbours and rivals of Athens and having suffered the effects of her often overbearing presence. However, the Spartans were unwilling to see the obliteration of a city that had taken the lead at Marathon and Salamis and, in a rare example of humanity rising above the bitterness of the lengthy war, vetoed the allies' demands. The exactions of the terms of a peace treaty that were decided upon were severe enough. Athens was to lose her foreign possessions and to demolish the long walls that gave her the security almost of an island and the walls of the Piraeus, and her fleet was to be confiscated or destroyed down to a limit of twelve ships, to allow her exiles to return and to count as friends and enemies the same people as the Spartans, and to follow Sparta by land or sea wherever she should go.

When Theramenes and his colleagues returned to Athens, he took the role of spokesman in the *ekklesia* and reported the terms on which the Spartans offered peace. With people dying of starvation, there was little opposition to his recommendation that the terms should be accepted, and the vote was passed accordingly. Then Lysander sailed into the Piraeus, and the Peloponnesian crews landed and began to tear down the walls, apparently with something of a carnival atmosphere, 'to the music of flute girls,' thinking that the day was 'the beginning of freedom for Greece.'

Lysander then continued his policy of installing oligarchic governments, previously in the islands that had been under democratic control, this time in the birthplace of democracy. He spoke in the *ekklesia,* demanding that the Athenians dissolve the democracy and appoint thirty men to 'frame a constitution based on the ancient laws under which to conduct the government.' This exposed the deep division between the democratic and much smaller, oligarchic factions. The latter, which included returned exiles and was by no means dismayed at the occupation by a foreign force politically sympathetic to them, claimed that a constitution based on 'the ancient laws' would be an oligarchy, as that was the form of government before the reforms of Kleisthenes. The democrats naturally claimed that democracy had been the Athenian form of government for a century and that it would be a terrible thing for them to lose their freedom. According to Diodorus Siculus, this sentiment was eloquently expressed by Theramenes, but this seems doubtful, as although a comparatively mild one, Theramenes was an oligarch, and it seems probable that his assumption of a leadership role in the peace negotiations was intended to provide him with a platform from which to re-establish a regime like that of the Five Thousand in which he had been a central figure. In any case, Lysander would not hear of a continuing democracy, and the *ekklesia* voted to terminate the democracy and to appoint thirty men to decide the nature of the doubtless oligarchic constitution to replace it.

The equanimity with which the peace was received by the oligarchs reinforced the suspicion that the series of events: the execution of the generals, in which Theramenes played a significant part, and which weakened the cadre of experienced naval commanders, and the inexplicable amateurishness of the handling of the fleet at Aigospotami, providing Lysander with a walkover, then the prominence of Theramenes in the peace negotiations, were all part of a deep oligarchic conspiracy to destroy Athens' democracy.

Chapter 12
The Rule and Overthrow of the Thirty

Lysander's fortuitous elimination of the greater part of the Athenian fleet, aided perhaps by the treachery of the oligarchic faction in Athens, had enabled him to starve the Athenians into submission. As a dedicated enemy of democracy, he applied his policy of installing oligarchic regimes wherever he overthrew democracies to the very birthplace of democracy in Athens, with the creation of the government of 'the Thirty,' being thirty individuals supposedly chosen by the Athenian assembly as being the most suited to guide Athens in its extremity as a defeated state, subject to the will of its Spartan conqueror.

The Thirty were, with perhaps one exception, extreme oligarchs, led by Kritias, a one-time friend and pupil of Socrates, who is the eponymous subject of a Platonic dialogue and also appears in the *Gorgias*, where he praises the idea of a retributive afterlife as helping to keep the lower classes in order. Kritias possessed a hatred of the proletariat, possibly unmatched until the Spanish Civil War. The one exception was the ubiquitous Theramenes, who had been a leading oligarch in the revolt of 411 BC but who had become a supporter of the democracy. (This had earned him the soubriquet of 'buskin': an over-boot that could be worn on either foot.) He had then served as a general in the navy and then again was the leader in the prosecution of the six generals after Arginusai and was possibly connected with a betrayal at Aigospotami. Theramenes had consistently held a position on the moderate wing of the oligarchic faction and, during the rule of the Four Hundred, had diverged from the extremists who were prepared to bring in a Spartan force to support them. After the end of the rule of the Four Hundred, he was the leading light in the Rule of the Five Thousand, which satisfied his ambition of having a government possessing elements both of democracy and oligarchy but which was unable to withstand the popular demand for the re-establishment of full, 'radical' democracy. Despite this disappointment, he was apparently reconciled to the democratic regime, actively engaged with the navy as a trierarch and a general. Theramenes was selected as one of the Thirty, being seen as a counter-weight to the extremists, particularly Kritias.

Following the same pattern as the Four Hundred, the Thirty were formally charged to devise a constitution which would return to the customs and conventions 'of their forefathers,' with the none too subtle intention of establishing an oligarchy. Despite this supposed role, the Thirty, following the example of the Four Hundred, 'continually delayed framing and publishing the new constitution' and set about ruling as if constitutionally authorised, appointing a *Boule* and various magistracies. They then undertook a purge of what many thought represented the worst aspects of the democracy, namely the 'sycophants,' or informers, and others who had 'been offensive to the aristocrats.' These were brought to trial by the *Boule*, found guilty and executed. This measure found general acceptance amongst the citizens, particularly, as Xenophon says, 'All who were conscious they were not of the same sort themselves.'

The Thirty clearly wished to extend their purging of what they regarded as undesirables far beyond the generally hated sycophants. Recognising that this might well require considerable coercive capabilities, they sent representatives to Lysander, now at Sparta, to ask him to help them secure the sending of a Spartan garrison, to 'help put the scoundrels out of the way and establish their government.' They agreed to pay for the maintenance of this garrison. Lysander, no doubt gladly, agreed to help them and seven hundred troops were duly dispatched under Callibius as governor or *harmost*. (The installation of Spartan garrisons, particularly where oligarchies had recently been assisted to take power by Lysander, was standard practice.) The Thirty made much of Callibius, bribing him to ensure his cooperation in their pursuit of the 'scoundrels' so that their arrests were accomplished with the assistance of guardsmen from the garrison. Initially, these were of those who were popular with the *demos,* and then wealthy citizens and metics executed to allow the confiscation of their estates, which they then shared out amongst themselves. One victim was Niceratos, the son of Nicias, the unfortunate commander of the Sicilian invasion, who had inherited his father's wealth as well as his public respect. His treatment caused considerable disquiet among the citizenry.

Theramenes protested in the *Boule* against the killing of men because they were 'honoured by the *demos*' but were doing no harm to society. Kritias called him a fool, despite their preceding friendship, for not wishing to 'put out of the way' people who were able to oppose the government of the Thirty. The killing went on, and the Thirty became aware of the number of citizens banding together to confront the reign of terror. Theramenes spoke again, saying that the oligarchy could not continue if they remained isolated from the citizens they were supposed to be ruling. Kritias' answer to this was to enroll three thousand citizens who would be permitted to possess arms and who supposedly were to participate in the government, while the rest were disarmed by the guardsmen and 'such citizens who were in sympathy with them.' The arms seized were deposited in the Acropolis. Theramenes objected to this move also on the grounds of the arbitrariness of the number, the fact that even with three thousand, they would be heavily outnumbered, and also that the city would be vulnerable to external attack with so many of its citizens disarmed. The enrolment was made even more divisive and threatening by a decree that removed any legal penalty for the killing by the state of a man not enrolled in the Three Thousand.

The reign of terror continued at an increased tempo, with particular emphasis on metics. Every one of the Thirty of the government was to seize a metic and have him put to death to permit the confiscation of his property, the money thus accrued to be used to pay the Spartan garrison. Theramenes was included in this allocation but refused, saying that these actions were worse than those of the sycophants that they had executed – at least they had let off with their lives those they accused. Theramenes' continual criticism of the thirty's actions persuaded many of them that he was an obstacle to their 'doing whatever they wanted to do.' A whispering campaign was started against him, and he was summoned to be tried by the *Boule*, with those intent on achieving a verdict against him resorting to the well-tried technique of hiring a pack of young men armed with daggers to attend the meeting. Kritias led the attack: 'Any change of government involves loss of life, that to oligarchy particularly because of the large number of enemies. We are against democracy, like the Spartans, so we invite them to assist us in establishing the oligarchy. If anyone opposes us, we put them out of the way, particularly if such is one of us. No one finds more fault with us than Theramenes, and he is not only an enemy but as a turncoat, a scoundrel.' Kritias went on to expatiate on Theramenes' reputation for changing sides: 'Although he began the cordial relations with the Spartans and was the very man starting the overthrow of the democracy, now he disapproves of what we are doing, so he can change sides again. So he is a traitor – the worst kind of villain. His past deeds: a leader of the Four Hundred, but seeing opposition was rising, became a champion of democracy – hence *buskin*. Also, he led the prosecution of the generals despite his responsibility for rescuing the wrecked sailors to save himself. I arraign him as a traitor. If you spare him, this will give others who oppose us high hopes, which must be destroyed.'

Theramenes then spoke. "I was in agreement with bringing the informers to trial, as many citizens agreed. But when they began to arrest men of worth and standing, I began to oppose them. Such was Niceratos son of Nicias. I objected also when the metics were arrested; it made them enemies also. I objected to the disarming of the citizens, as weakening the city, and the hiring of the garrison, which could have been done by a similar number of citizens." He pointed out that the banishment of the democracy-supporting Thrasybulus, Anytus and Alcibiades had simply served to strengthen the leadership of the democrats. He then returned to the illegal killing: "It is not I who are turning the populace against us, but those who are killing and robbing those who have done no wrong." Finally, he turned on Kritias: "Kritias calls me buskin, but he pleases neither party – he was the bitterest of all haters of the *demos*, now in the oligarchy, he is the bitterest hater of the better classes."

The *Boule* received Theramenes' *apologia* well, and Kritias recognised that a vote would set him free. So he went out to fetch the young men with daggers to stand in the council chamber and intimated that they would not permit Theramenes to go free. He reminded members of the *Boule* that anyone not on the roll of the three thousand could be condemned to death by the Thirty without a vote. He then pronounced Theramenes as being struck off the roll, and that being done, he announced that he was condemned to death. Theramenes mounted the altar in the council room, maintaining that he was not expecting sanctuary, to which he was entitled, but to emphasise the fact that the Thirty 'were not only unjust to men but impious to the gods.' Kritias then sent for the agents of the Eleven (the magistrates responsible for state executions) and had Theramenes dragged from the altar, despite Socrates' attempt to prevent this, and delivered to them, saying that he had been 'condemned according to the law,' and directing them to take him for execution. As Theramenes was dragged through the marketplace, he loudly protested against his unjust treatment. On being threatened that if he did not keep quiet, he would suffer for it, he replied that he was going to suffer anyway. Having drunk the hemlock, he threw the last few drops on the ground, saying, 'Here's to the health of my beloved Kritias.'

Theramenes' judicial murder was a sign of the increasing isolation and desperation of the Thirty, and his reference to Thrasybulus would have reminded them, if such a reminder was necessary, of the appearance of a small but rapidly growing band of democrats, led by the trierarch and ex-general. Thrasybulus, surprisingly in view of his wealth and well-known democratic sympathies, had been banished rather than executed, although his estate had been confiscated. Along with a number of fellow democrats, he had been welcomed in Thebes as a gesture of defiance against the Spartans, who had annoyed the Thebans by their overbearing attitude. As the feeling against the Thirty became stronger, he deemed the time right for an attempt to overthrow the oligarchy and re-establish democracy, and with some seventy supporters, established himself in a well-defended fortress at Phyle on the Parnes mountain range near the Boeoetian border, about thirteen miles north of Athens.

The Thirty were keen to eradicate this threat and called up some of the enrolled arms-bearing Three Thousand, together with some cavalry (who appear to have been their most committed supporters), led by a few of their own number, and advanced up to the fortress at Phyle. Some of the more adventurous attempted an immediate attack and were driven off with some casualties. Cooler heads proposed a more conventional approach, to block the democrats' access to supplies by guarding the tracks to the fortress, but during the night, there was an unseasonable heavy snowstorm, and the enterprise was abandoned with the force returning to the city having lost a few of their number. The Thirty were loath to leave the democrats to their own devices, able to obtain supplies from the local farms, and so sent out most of the Spartan garrison and two divisions of cavalry, who made camp in the evening a couple of miles from Phyle. Thrasybulus then led his force, now considerably increased in size, against the Spartans and oligarchs, marching during the night and taking them by surprise as they got up at dawn, variously attending to calls of nature in the surrounding woodland or currying the horses, killing more than 120 hoplites and cavalrymen with the survivors taking to flight. Thrasybulus was then emboldened to move closer to the city and installed his force in the

Piraeus, the home of the fleet and the democratic naval tradition.

When the Thirty became aware of the closeness of the democratic force, they realised that the survival of the oligarchy was under severe threat and that drastic action was necessary. Accordingly, they assembled all the forces available to them, including the Spartan guardsmen and their own cavalry and hoplites, and sent them off along the road to the Piraeus under the command of Kritias. The men from Phyle initially attempted to halt them on the road but realised that their numbers were insufficient. They then retreated to the hill of Munichia in the Piraeus, at the crest of which they formed a compact body blocking the road leading to the temple of Artemis, which occupies the summit. Thrasybulus gave a rousing speech in which he congratulated his force on this opportunity to take vengeance on 'those who had stolen their city from them' and assured them of victory despite their small numbers, predicting that the attacking oligarchs would be at a great disadvantage fighting up the hill, as that they would unable to throw missiles. By contrast, the democrats were well provided with javelin men and *peltasts* who were able to launch their darts and stones over the heads of their comrades, outweighing their disadvantage in the number of hoplites. As Thrasybulus had predicted, their positional advantage gave them victory over the oligarchy's force, in which Critias was killed, having deliberately chosen to place himself at the extreme right end of the phalanx, the most dangerous position, being unprotected by the shield of a man on his right hand. After the battle, there was considerable fraternisation between the two sides, now under a truce. The herald Cleocritus, from the side of the 'men of Piraeus,' called on the oligarchic force to abandon their allegiance to the Thirty, reminding them of their common backgrounds as citizens of Athens, pointing out that the Thirty had killed nearly more Athenians in their eight months of rule than the Peloponnesians in the entire war. The surviving officials of the Thirty rapidly shepherded their forces away before rebellion broke out.

The Three Thousand, having been enrolled by the Thirty as a guarantee of their connection with the Athenian citizenry, lost patience with their oligarchic leaders after this latest defeat and, in a gathering of a significant number, voted to depose them. The Thirty, recognising that their continued presence in the city was unwise, decamped to Eleusis, where they had prepared a refuge, incidentally killing some three hundred of the inhabitants. The Three Thousand, who still supported an oligarchic government and were concerned to prevent civic disturbance, voted in a council of ten, one man from each tribe, who would police the city with the cavalry commanders. Then followed a period of desultory skirmishing, during which the men of Piraeus – the democrats – whose numbers were increasing daily, roamed the hinterland in search of supplies while the remains of the three thousand ventured nowhere without the accompaniment of the cavalry. Occasionally, the democrats would be caught by the cavalry and sustain casualties, and the cavalry commander Lysimachus distinguished himself by slaughtering some farmers who were attempting to reach their own farms.

The Thirty, in their effective exile at Eleusis, once again turned to Lysander, sending ambassadors to plead for his assistance on the grounds that the democrats had revolted against the terms of the peace treaty, having caused numerous casualties amongst the Spartan guardsmen. Lysander, as ever, was keen to act against the democrats and perhaps surprisingly persuaded the Spartan government to make him governor of Athens on land, supported by a force of mercenaries, and his brother Libys, admiral of a fleet, sent to blockade the Piraeus. At the same time, they lent the oligarchs 100 Talents. The future looked grim for the men of Piraeus. At this juncture, however, salvation of a sort appeared in the surprising form of one of the two Spartan kings, Pausanias. Pausanias, in common with many Spartans, particularly those of the upper echelons of society, was not an admirer of Lysander despite his undoubted military prowess. Lysander had never hidden his belief that his achievements should have compensated for his deeply resented exclusion from royal status and had become unpopular for his haughty behaviour. Having been an honoured guest at the court of the son of the Persian king was hardly likely to have instilled any tendency to humility, and Pausanias was unwilling to permit him to augment further his reputation as the conqueror of Athens, and his policy from the start appears to have been to bring about a reconciliation between the 'men of the city' – the oligarchs, and the men of Piraeus – the democrats, rather than indulging in an extended celebration of revenge against the largely democratic Athens which had fought against Sparta. He had persuaded a majority of the ephors that he should lead a Spartan force to Athens for this purpose, with Lysander being reduced to a subordinate role.

On arriving, Pausanias led his joint force with him, commanding the right wing, manned by the Spartans and their allies, while Lysander led the left wing, manned by mercenaries, and approached the Piraeus. He sent ambassadors to the men in Piraeus, urging them to disperse to their homes. When they refused to go, he led a half-hearted advance, having raised the paean, then retired, 'having achieved nothing' but a display of force. On the next day, he returned to the coast and advanced with a mixed force of Spartans and Athenian cavalry and reconnoitred, to see if a wall could cut the Piraeus off. He was attacked by men from the Piraeus, causing some casualties, and 'becoming angry' ordered the cavalry into the attack, followed up by some of his infantry, killing some thirty of the enemy and chasing the rest back to their lair in the Piraeus. Then Thrasybulus and the rest of the force in the Piraeus came out and formed up to confront Pausanias' force. The ensuing fight, being somewhat unequal, ended with the Democrats losing about 150. Pausanias then set up a trophy and returned to his camp.

Despite these hostilities, Pausanias clearly wished to avoid further conflict. He sent word to the men in the Piraeus to send ambassadors to him with their proposals for peace, with recommendations as to what they should say. Thrasybulus, recognising that further armed conflict was unlikely to succeed, agreed to this and the ambassadors were sent. Pausanias also gathered men from the city who wished to end the factional war and were prepared to tell him and the ephors with him that they had no desire for warfare with the men in Piraeus and wished to be reconciled with them and in common with them be friends of the Spartans, and that they and the men from Piraeus should send ambassadors to Sparta for their proposals to be heard. The ephors who had travelled with Pausanias were of a like mind with him, rather than Lysander, and welcomed the prospect of reconciliation and sent the envoys both from Piraeus and the city with their proposals for peace. After the Athenian envoys had been heard by the Spartan assembly, they sent fifteen men to Athens to join Pausanias, commissioned to effect a reconciliation 'in the best way they could.' The subsequent agreement required the two parties, the city and the Piraeus, to live in peace with each other and that every man should depart to his home except for the Thirty, the ten who had previously been put in charge of the Piraeus by them and the eleven who had carried out executions on the instructions of the Thirty. Those who were unhappy or unwilling to stay should go to Eleusis. With these terms agreed by the two factions, Pausanias disbanded his army and dismissed them to their various cities.

Following a visit by the democrats to the Acropolis, where they offered sacrifices, an assembly was convened. At this, according to Xenophon, Thrasybulus spoke, directing his thoughts to the 'Men of the City' – the supporters of the oligarchy – contrasting their 'disgraceful' behaviour in pursuit of gain with that of the *demos* who, despite their poverty, 'never did wrong for the sake of money.' In like vein, he compared the military advantages possessed by the oligarchs: 'arms, money and the Peloponnesians as allies,' while the *demos* had none of these, and yet they were victorious. Given this, the 'Men of the City' had no cause for arrogance. Indeed, a degree of humility would be appropriate. He made it clear that there would be no retribution, and they should not be afraid, but that they should be true to the oaths they had sworn in accepting the terms of the reconciliation 'as god-fearing men,' and that they would only have to live under the laws that had previously been in force: those of the democracy. With this, he dismissed the assembly.

Xenophon's narrative is both highly compressed and factually inaccurate – the return of democracy was a somewhat more complex affair than he describes, and Thrasybulus, despite his leading role in the overthrow of the Thirty, played a comparatively minor part in the re-establishment of the democratic constitution. It does, however, capture the remarkable forbearance of the democratic victors, who agreed to an amnesty for all except the thirty themselves and their immediate henchmen, which was respected almost without exception. One distinctly sour note was struck by the *ekklesia* under the influence of Archinos, who indicted Thrasybulus for proposing that 'those who had had a part in the return from the Piraeus' should be granted citizenship. This is applauded by Aristotle in the *Constitution of Athens* because some of these 'were manifestly slaves.' Some two years after the re-establishment of the democracy, it was learnt that the oligarchs who had set up a statelet in Eleusis were recruiting mercenaries, and a force was sent to confront them. A conference was arranged for the generals of both sides; those from Eleusis were seized and put to death, signalling that the patience of the democrats was not unlimited. The oligarchs were then persuaded to accept reconciliation, and many returned to the city.

Thus, the democratic constitution was re-established, the occupation by foreign troops was ended, and, amazingly, considering the bitterness of the factional struggle, the citizenry returned to living at peace with each other. A situation that was to last for some eighty years. The Athenians, however, had lost both their empire and their navy – the essential underpinnings of democracy. The loss of the *phoros* payments left the city's finances in a parlous state, one that would place ever-increasing demands on the wealthy and not-so-wealthy, who were used to only rare exactions. (Despite this, the democratic regime assumed the debt incurred by the Thirty in requesting the Spartan garrison and paid it in full.) The loss of the navy – reduced to only twelve ships – left Athens vulnerable, particularly to her grain supply, and also removed the essential role of the *thetes* as the source of the navy's manpower and, with it, their self-confidence as the front-line defenders of the state.

A question mark hangs over the Spartan King Pausanias, who played a pivotal role in this restoration, specifically: what was his motivation? Athens was Sparta's main rival, and although the Spartans had refused the demands of the Corinthians and Thebans to destroy the city, showing a level of humanity already commented upon, it might have been thought both just and expedient to weaken her by encouraging the divisions that were so apparent following the end of the war, as Lysander had intended. Instead, Pausanias had worked to unite the two factions despite considerable provocations, knowing that the result would be the restoration of democracy – a form of government that the Spartans traditionally despised. The ancient writers explain his actions as the result of jealousy of Lysander, possibly mixed with regal disdain. Yet, it is difficult to accept this as a complete explanation. One possible contributory factor was the disgraceful behaviour of the Spartan-supported Thirty in their brief and bloody reign. This had been only one example, although the extreme one, that typified the way in which the other oligarchies that Lysander had installed ruled, with massacres of their opponents, confiscations and exile, supported by Spartan force. There was at least some recognition in Sparta that these reflected badly on her, particularly in that Sparta had entered the Peloponnesian war supposedly to 'free the Greeks' and could be accused of replacing Athenian imperial tyranny with her own.

Epilogue

Athens' democracy had been saved by a combination of the unflinching democrats, personified by Thrasybulus, who had fought against the tyrannical Thirty and their allies, and the remarkable forbearance and humanity of Pausanias, the Spartan king. The terms of the peace agreement, however, closely supervised by the Spartans, left the state as a shadow of its former self, stripped of its empire and effectively its navy – the custodian of its power and protection. With these gone, went also the major source of its wealth. Practically, the only redeeming feature was the absence of vengeance and retribution against those who had failed to support democracy, except, perhaps, in the case of the philosopher Socrates.

The trial of Socrates has been seen by some as an indication of the decline in the moral standing of the democratic regime following the Peloponnesian war; his subsequent execution characterised as a barbaric attack on the freedom of thought of which he has become a martyred symbol. The main accusation against Socrates was that of corrupting youth, often as instilling in his many youthful followers a lack of respect for their elders and their beliefs, as demonstrated by their questioning of conventional views. Another suggestion concentrates rather on some of the individuals who were associated with him, notably

Kritias, the fanatical leader of the Thirty, and also Alcibiades, whose undoubted military abilities, which did so much to re-vitalise the democracy following the oligarchic revolt, for many failed to outweigh the suspicions of impiety involved in the mutilation of the herms, also his role in the Sicilian disaster, and his frequently expressed contempt for democracy at various stages of his career. Another of Socrates' associates was Theramenes, who played a dishonourable part in the trial of the generals after Arginusai, and then was a member of the Thirty, albeit a dissenting voice, one that Kritias rewarded with death. In the events leading up to Theramenes' death, Socrates appears in a hopeless attempt to prevent him being dragged from the altar. This is surprising as the event took place in a meeting of the *Boule*, which had been assembled by the Thirty and consisted of their 'personal cronies' according to Diodorus, which suggests that Socrates was one of these. It is possible, then, that Socrates was accused essentially because of his association and, by implication, his influence with those who were anti-democrats. It might also be noted that one of his accusers was Anytus, who was one of the leaders of the democrats against the Thirty. If this was the explanation, Socrates' execution was perhaps rather more understandable than has been maintained.

It might have been thought that the end of the Peloponnesian war would have heralded an epoch of peace in Greece; however, this was far from being the case. The Spartans, buoyed up by their victory and the reclaiming of their hegemony, were eager to demonstrate their power, and one of their joint kings, Agesileos, was determined to project this power against the most obvious rival – Persia. In an unusual venture for the Spartans, who were notoriously reluctant to act outside the confines of Greece, he led an expedition to the Persian-controlled Eastern coast of the Aegean and took several significant cities. The Persian response to this reflected their growing sophistication in their dealings with Greek states and formed a coalition against Sparta, consisting of Athens, Corinth, Thebes and Argos. (The composition of this alliance illustrated the changed allegiances that had occurred in the few years after the Peloponnesian war, in that Corinth and Thebes had been hostile to Athens, and Corinth particularly had been a close ally of Sparta.) The resulting conflict became known as the Corinthian War and involved both land and sea battles, with the Athenians, bereft of their navy, involved only on land.

A surprising interjection into this conflict was provided by the Athenian naval commander Konon, who had escaped from the disaster at Aegospotami and sailed with eight ships to Cyprus, where he was welcomed by its ruler Evagoras. On learning that the Persians were building up a fleet to oppose the Spartans, who had overcome their previous inferiority in marine warfare, Konon volunteered his abilities to the Persians and was put in charge of their new naval force. In a sign of the growing dissatisfaction under the terms of the peace treaty, considerable numbers of Athenians who had served in their navy made their way to join Konon in his new command. This led to a daring exploit by one Demaenetos, who made off with one of the few triremes left to the Athenians to sail to join Konon. The fact that the launching of a trireme from its ramp in a trireme shed took a considerable number of men and that it would appear that the ship was fully manned, as it attacked another ship, probably Aeginetan, on its escape, and the crew, finding that it was in better condition than the one they had taken, hi-jacked it, suggests that the Athenian authorities turned a blind eye to the escapade. This, in turn, led to a factional split in the Athenian assembly between those who were afraid of provoking the Spartans and the 'war faction,' who were less concerned and were accused of seeking to re-open hostilities with Sparta.

In 394 BC, Konon led his Persian fleet to victory against the Spartans at Knidos and then sailed to the Piraeus, where his crews helped to rebuild the walls leading to the city, which had been pulled down on the orders of Lysander. These events restored confidence to the Athenians, who felt that a weakened Sparta would be unable to enforce the terms of the peace treaty, and they returned to rebuilding their fleet and to envisage re-establishing their naval power. By 390 BC, their confidence had recovered to such an extent that the democratic hero Thrasybulos set off with a small force of ships to visit some of the subjects of the empire in the hope of obtaining money. He was successful at Thasos and then sailed to Aspendos, on the river Eurymedon, the scene of Kimon's great victory over the Persians. Here, he also persuaded the authorities to provide money and retired to his ship anchored in the river. Unfortunately, some of the crews of his ships decided to attempt some free-lance fee-gathering, and the outraged inhabitants attacked the Athenian force. And Thrasybulos was killed in his tent on the river bank. A sad end to such a brave and principled man.

The Spartans inevitably became disturbed at Athens' growing confidence and naval resources, to such an extent that they began to send ships to the Hellespont to threaten the Athenians' grain supply, following Lysander's successful tactic, although they refrained from imposing a complete blockade. Having reached somewhat of a deadlock, both sides appealed to the Persian king, Artaxerxes, for assistance against the other. The king's response, in line with the general antipathy felt by the Persian monarchy to Athens, was to impose what became known as 'The King's Peace.' This heavily favoured the Spartans, who were effectively to act as agents of the king, particularly in preventing Athens from attempting to re-establish her empire, being permitted only to retain the islands of Imbros and Lemnos, which had long been under Athens' control. As part of the King's Peace, there were to be no changes to the status of the Greek Ionian cities on the East Aegean coast and litoral, which remained firmly under Persian control. The Spartans' acquiescence to this did little to augment the validity of their proud boast of 'saving the Greeks from slavery.'

Despite their supposed custodianship of the peace, in 379 BC, the Spartans attacked the city of Thebes and installed a *harmost* – governor – and a garrison there. They were welcomed by a faction in the city, but the majority of the population were hostile, and after a short time, they revolted against the invaders and made them withdraw in a humiliating climb-down. This incident triggered a new sense of assertiveness in Thebes, and indeed the Boeotion state, which was to culminate in the establishing of a new hegemony – the Theban Hegemony – in Greece, with profound results for Sparta. Perhaps surprisingly, the Athenians did not welcome this development initially, even going so far as to execute an Athenian who had helped in the expulsion of the Spartans. Perhaps this was born from a combination of the long-standing enmity between Athens and Thebes, recently lessened to a certain extent, and a reluctance to disturb the King's Peace. However, this sentiment was rudely shattered by a bizarre incident in which a Spartan, one Sphodrias, led an expedition to attack the Piraeus. He got no further than Eleusis and was recalled by the Spartan authorities, but the Athenians took this as a breach of the peace and turned both to the support of the Thebans and also to initiate the development of a second league.

In the creation of the Athenians' second league, they at least initially tried to avoid the imperialistic behaviour that had led to them being widely hated as their empire developed. The league was supervised by a council containing representatives of the members, which met regularly, and its stated objective was 'to ensure that the Spartans allowed the Greeks to live in peace,' a formulation no doubt intended to point up the hypocrisy of the Spartans' old claim to be protecting the Greeks from slavery. The league was, again, a naval alliance strongly dependent on the Athenian navy, which was recovering something like its last-century strength. The navy was still supported by the trierarchy, although it was common for a ship to be financed by two or more trierarchs per year as the result of the general decline in the wealth of the city. The ships were still crewed largely by Athenian citizens, and, in a new development, experienced crewmen were recorded on rolls in a manner similar to those for hoplites and cavalrymen. The membership of the second league contained a number of states that had been in the Delian League, with others including even Thebes, despite its absence of any connection with the sea. The navy, commanded by the admiral Timotheos, successfully engaged with the Spartan fleet in a number of battles.

The assertiveness of the Thebans continued under the influence of their leading general, Epaminondas. In 371 BC, the Spartans decided that their pre-eminence was becoming threatened, and they attacked Thebes. The resulting battle at Leuctra was a crushing defeat for the Spartans by the Thebans under Epaminondas, which left the Thebes as the most powerful state in Greece. The Athenians, in turn, became disturbed by Thebes' new status and, in a remarkable development, offered support to their historic rivals and allied with Sparta. Epaminondas pursued a campaign to reduce Sparta's influence by visiting her allies during a number of invasions of the Peloponnesus. Eventually, Epaminondas attacked the Spartans at Mantinea in 362 BC. The result, again, was a crushing defeat for the Spartans, who lost so many men that they were finished as a force in Greece. However,

Epaminondas himself was killed, and the Theban hegemony was found to have been dependent on this one brilliant general. Although the Thebans retained a significant military force, they had lost the desire for domination, and Greece, for a while, was free from large-scale warfare. Despite being on the losing side at Mantinea, the Athenians were left as the least diminished of the previously recognised Greek hegemons.

As implied by the previous remark, this state of peace, or exhaustion, did not endure for long. The Athenians, despite their good intentions, had trouble with their second league when the islands of Rhodes, Chios, and Byzantium, all of which were strategically important to Athens' grain supply, had revolutions that replaced their democratic governments with oligarchies who promptly announced their intention to secede from the league. The resulting 'Social' war practically bankrupted Athens. However, a far more significant new threat to the established order arrived in the person of Philip of Macedon and the Macedonian army that he led. The Macedonians were generally regarded as close to barbarians by the rest of the Greeks. They drank their wine undiluted, and their dialect was largely unintelligible.

Furthermore, they had been essentially a nation of herders and farmers but had been converted to a militaristic state under the influence of a warlike royal monarchy, which was then more than a match for the enfeebled previous Greek hegemons. The Athenians attempted to counteract Phillip's all-too-obvious territorial ambitions with constant encouragement from the orator

Demosthenes, who never ceased to urge confrontation. Athens' currently straightened circumstances, however, precluded any large-scale military campaign, although on the rare occasions that Phillip ventured sea-going actions, the threat of the Athenian navy was enough to dissuade him. Eventually, the Athenians allied with Thebes and, in 338 BC, fought Phillip's army at Chaeronea. The result was a victory for Phillip and for the Thebans and Athenians, the realisation that their hegemonic days were over. Phillip dealt harshly with the Thebans, installing a Macedonian garrison in their city, but was comparatively merciful to Athens, possibly because he had ideas about using the Athenian fleet to transport his army to attack Persia. It was always the case that Phillip had a respect for Athenian culture and, within limits, had attempted to create, if not an alliance, an understanding with Athens. Under the influence of Demosthenes, however, the Athenians remained suspicious of his motives.

Phillip was assassinated in 435 BC and was succeeded by his son Alexander, not without some conflict with his family in the shape of a half-brother who possibly had a better claim to the throne. On his accession to the kingship, Alexander was surrounded by enemies, both domestic and national, in the sense of hostile Greek states, particularly the Thebans, but also several others. In a series of brilliant actions, often using highly unusual tactics, he defeated or reduced to passivity all his opponents and was left as the unchallenged ruler of Greece. On the whole, his brief sojourn in Greece in this commanding position was comparatively benign, with the exception of Thebes, which had been a consistent enemy both of his father and him, and he took severe revenge, destroying the city. Following Phillip's tendency, Alexander entertained a respect for Athens, possibly reinforced by Phillip's appointment of the philosopher Aristotle as his tutor. Aristotle was not an Athenian, and he was critical of democracy, but he was deeply involved in the philosophical culture of the city and would no doubt have attempted to inculcate some of this into his pupil.

After a short time, the extent of Alexander's ambition was too great to be restricted to the confines of Greece, and he assembled a large army with the intention of undertaking an expedition that was to enter Asia (as the term was then understood, now known as Asia Minor) via the Persian empire, and then penetrate Western Asia, as far as India, and also Egypt. His underlying motivation was to unite East and West under an imperial sway. Once the great conquest had begun, he was never to return to Greece.

After Alexander's premature death, the Athenians, as ever led on by the indefatigable Demosthenes, decided that this was the time to throw off Macedonian rule, at that time under the direction of Antipater, one of Phillip's generals. The Athenians gathered a force, including a number of allies, particularly Boeotians, and attacked Antipater's mainly Macedonian occupying army. They achieved minor success initially, but then Antipater rallied his troops with reinforcements and defeated the Athenians and their allies. Rather surprisingly, Antipater, who was a straightforward military man with little of Phillip's respect for the culture of Athens, refrained from destroying the city, but when he took personal control, he followed the example of Lysander and abolished the democracy in the form that had survived for nearly a century and a half. However, rather than installing a murderous clique of oligarchs, he insisted upon the restriction of full civic rights to a property-owning section of the populace, specifically, those whose property was worth at least two thousand drachma. This, of course, amongst others, removed the right to vote in the assembly from much of the *thetes* class and also negated the connection between the citizenry and the navy. Ironically, this form of limited democracy would have found favour with Aristotle and indeed resembled the 'Rule of the Five Thousand' that followed the oligarchic revolt of 411 BC as instigated by Theramenes and praised by Thucydides.

As the end of the fourth century BC approached, Athens retained much of its culture; its architectural magnificence had, if anything had, been enhanced; although the era of great tragedy had passed, the 'new comedy' found widespread popularity, with imitators in Rome, and the city's reputation as a centre of philosophical thought was to flourish for several centuries. What, of course, was lacking was the spirit deriving from the universal suffrage of the democratic regime. Pericles' proud boast in the *epitaphios logos* that Athens was the 'school for the whole of Greece' might well still be true for the beauty of its buildings, its poets, playwrights and philosophers, but no longer for civic pride based on the potential involvement of every (male) citizen in the governance of the state. That said, there is no doubt that Athenian culture survived the fading of the hegemonic pre-eminence of the city and, indeed, was carried into Asia in the numerous cities that Alexander founded throughout his journey of conquest and was maintained by the Roman Eastern Empire, throughout which Greek was the *lingua franca*.